Artwork of Pat Reed

Pat, you've truly inspired and touched so many people's lives, thank you.

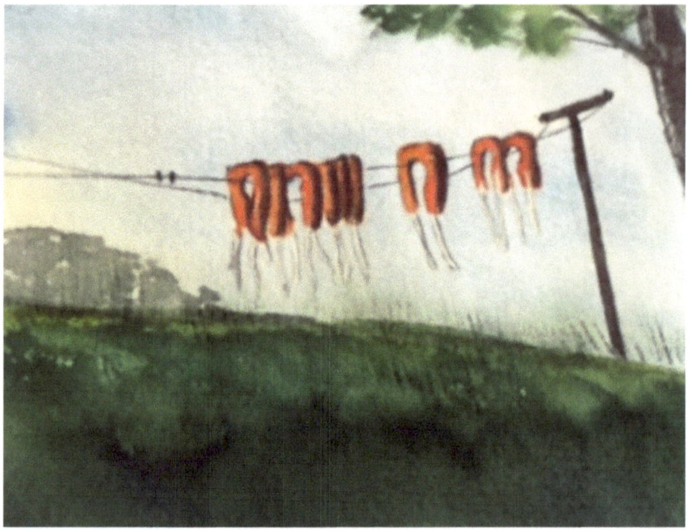

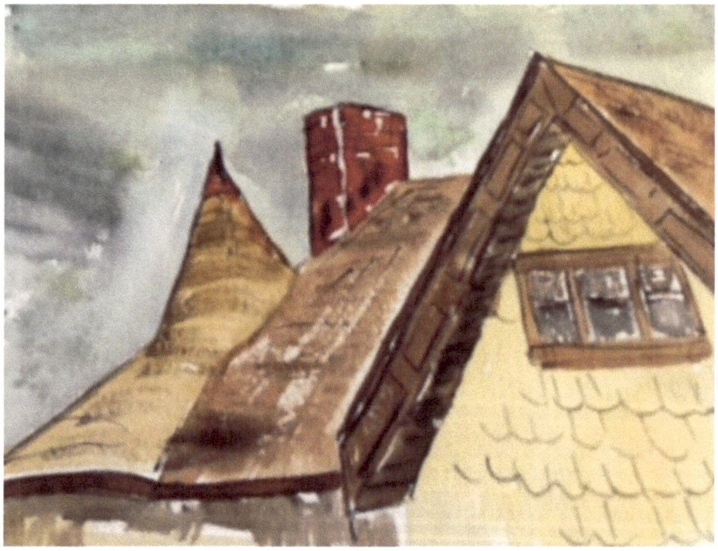

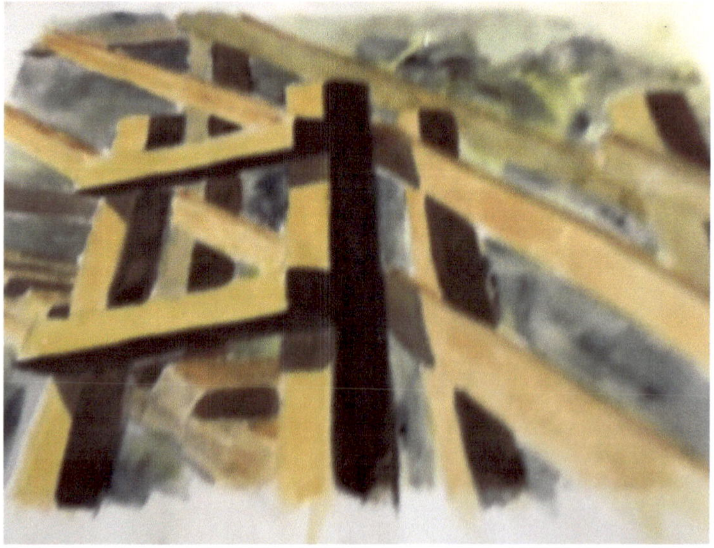

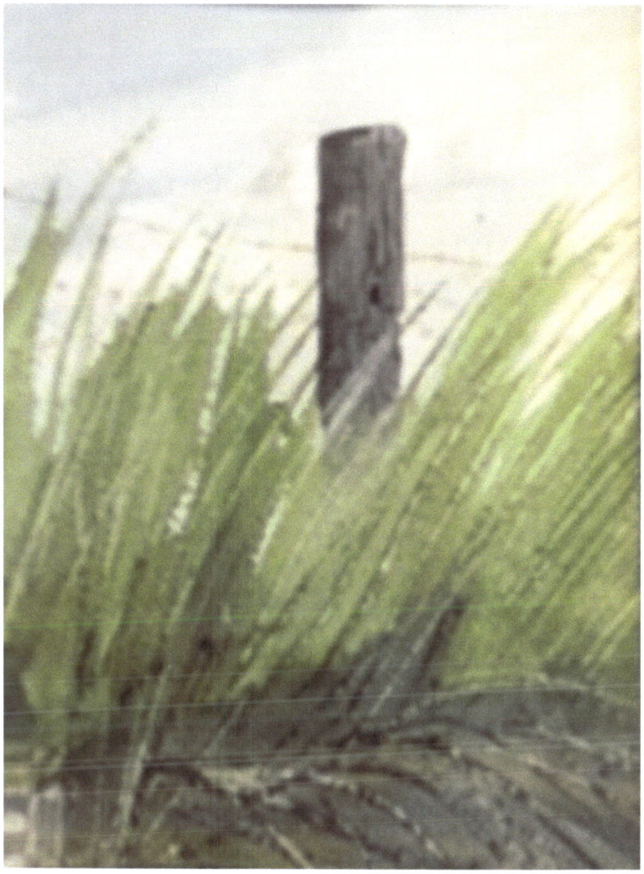
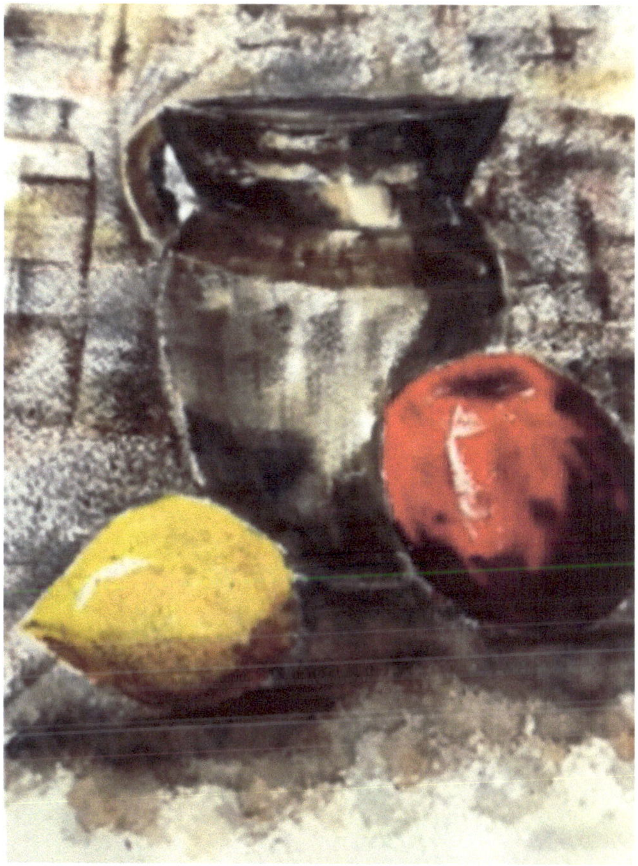
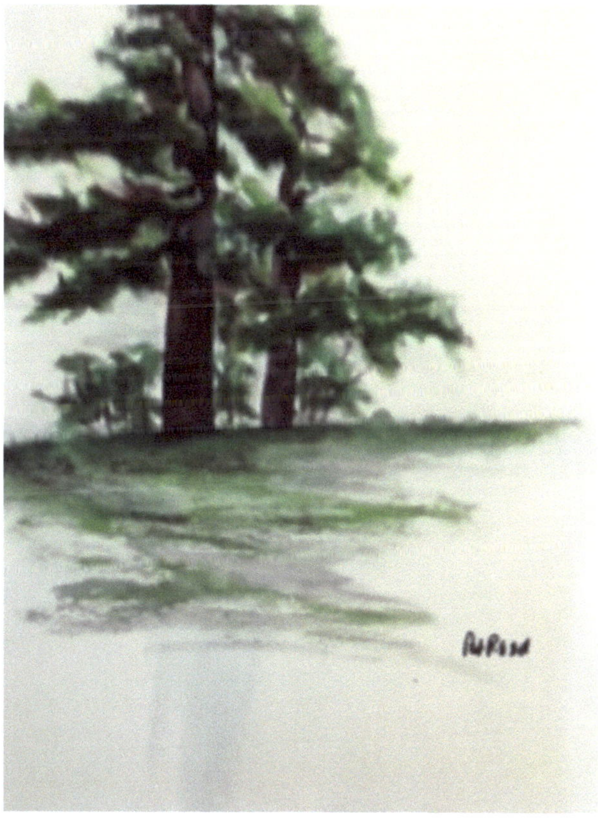

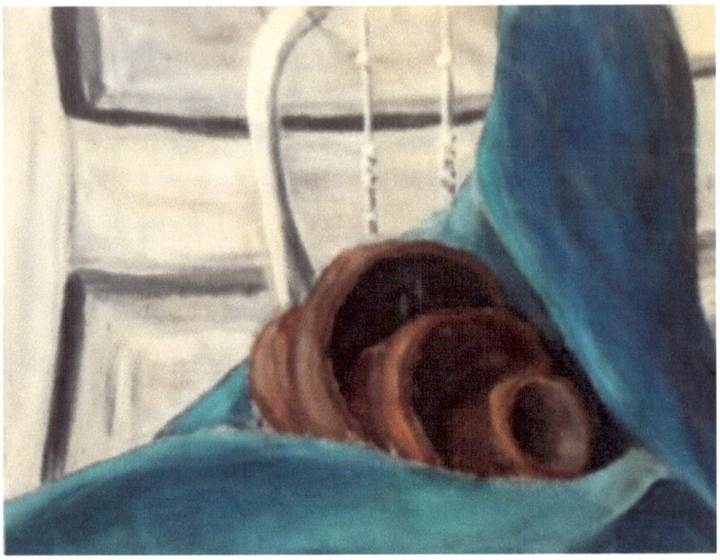

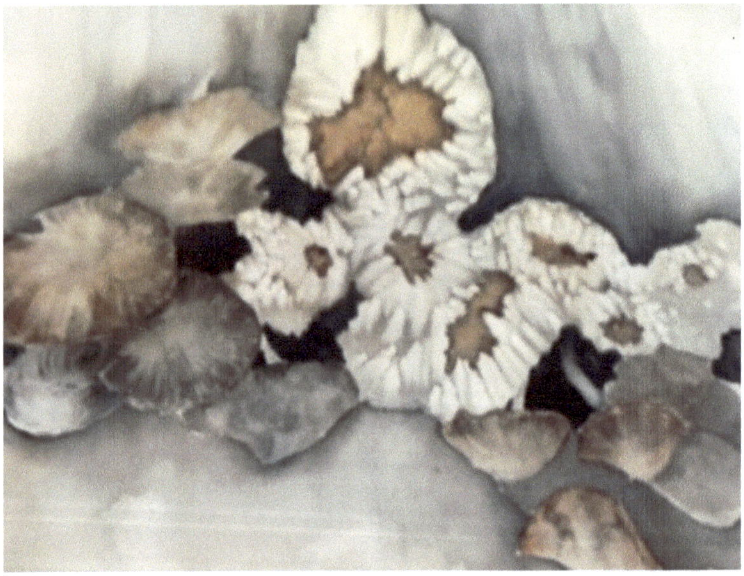

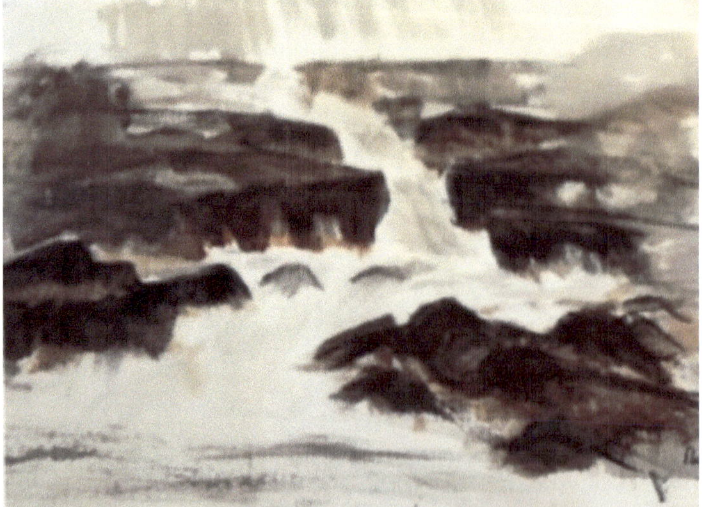

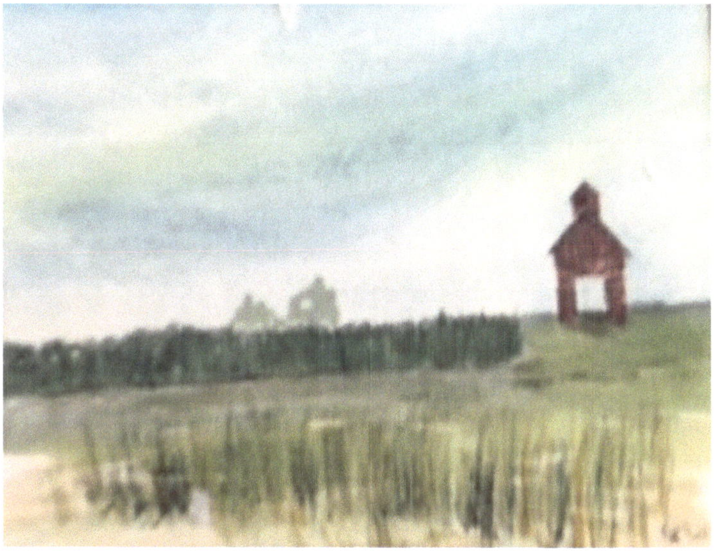

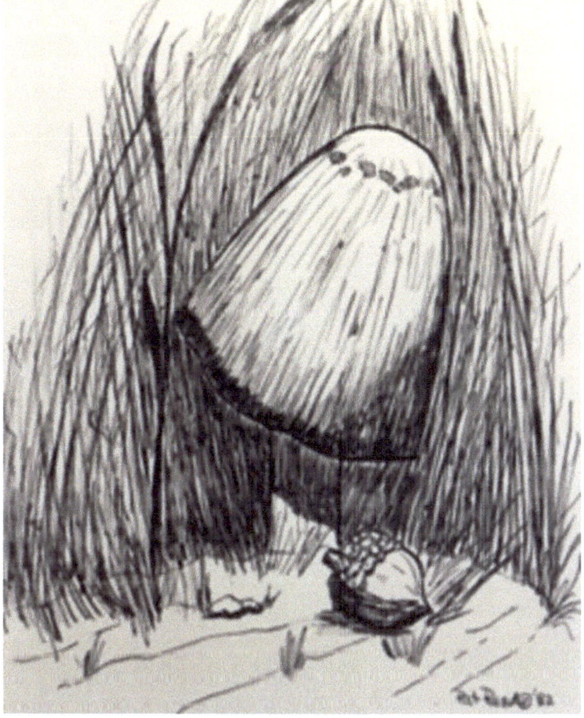

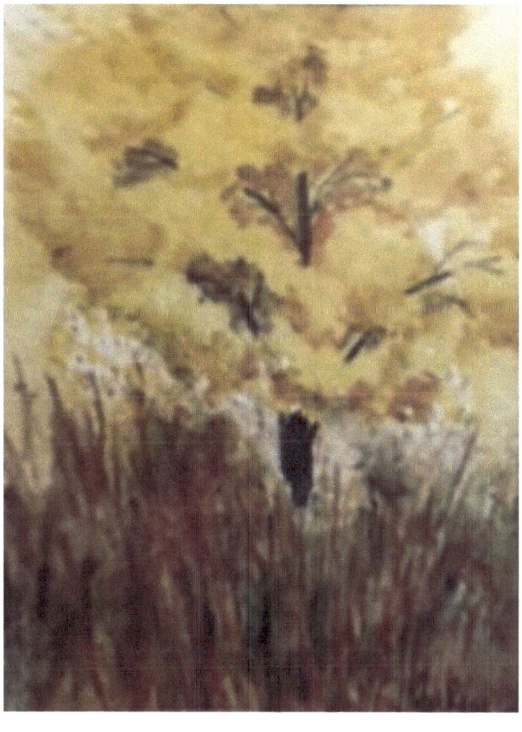

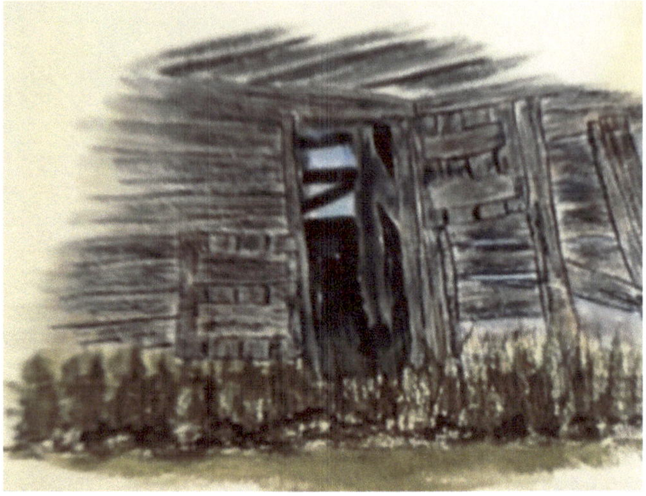

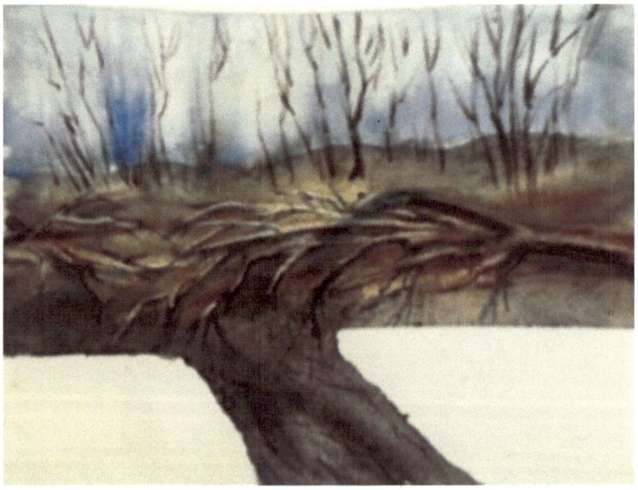

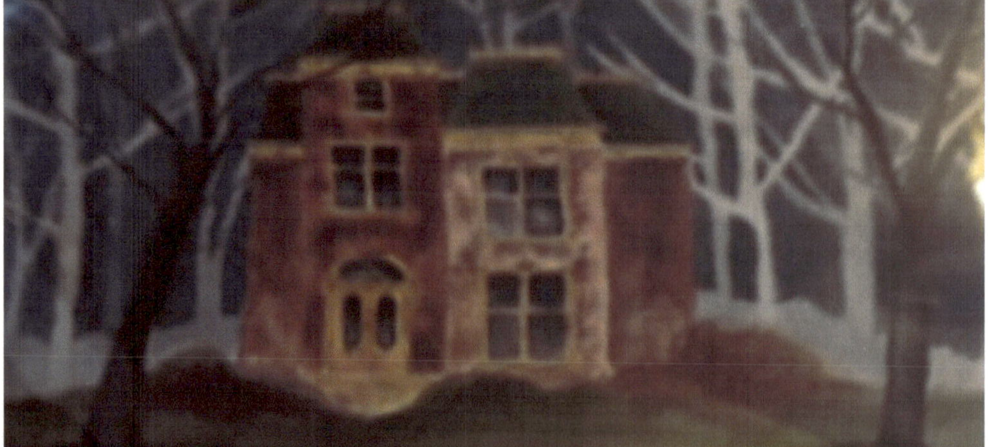

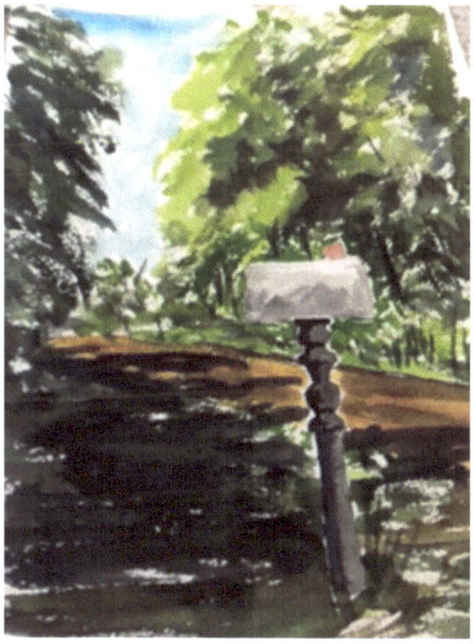

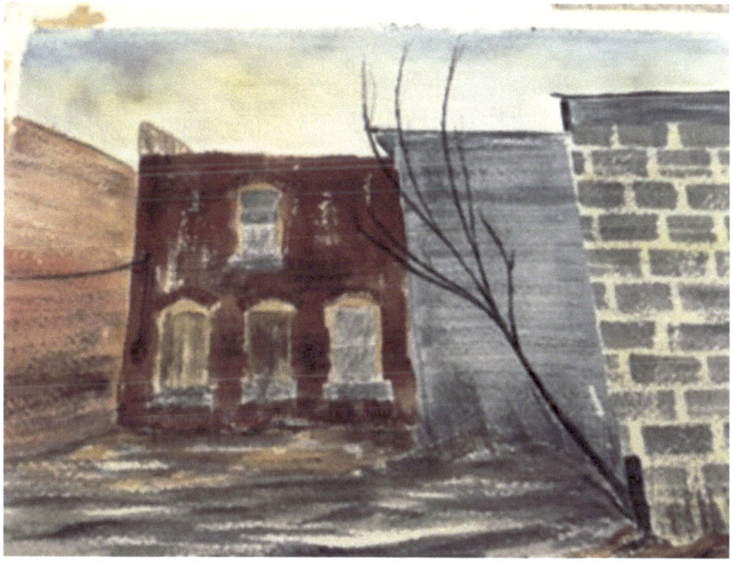

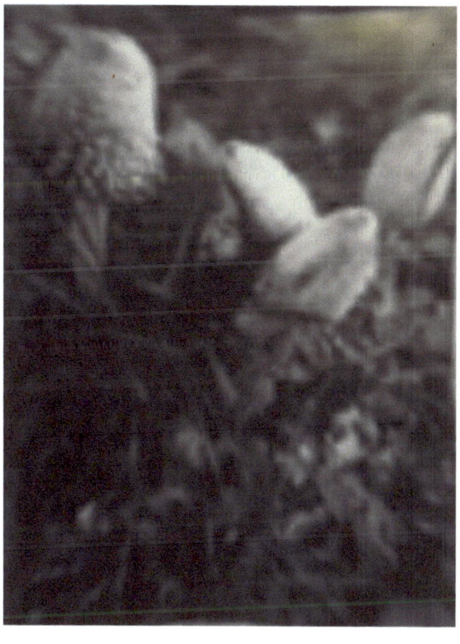

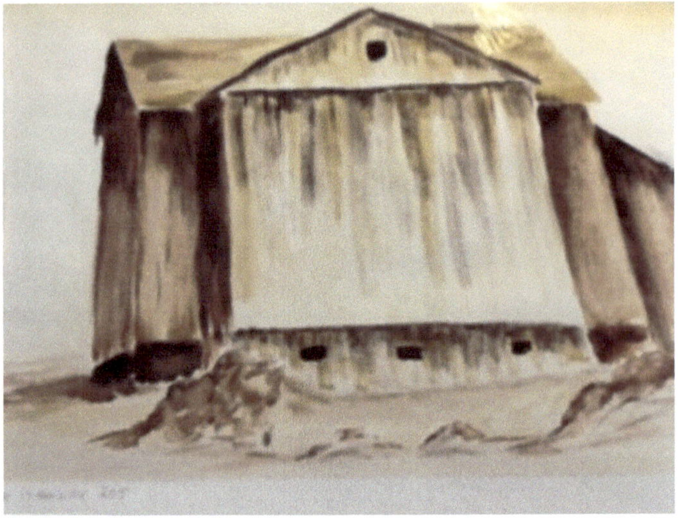

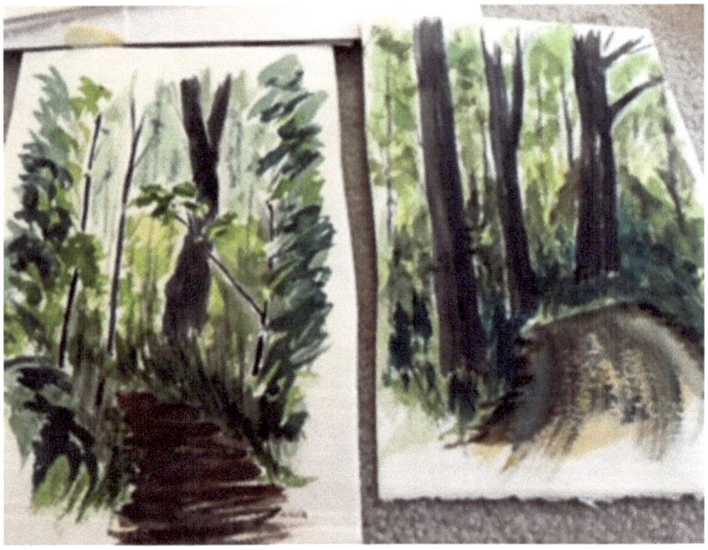

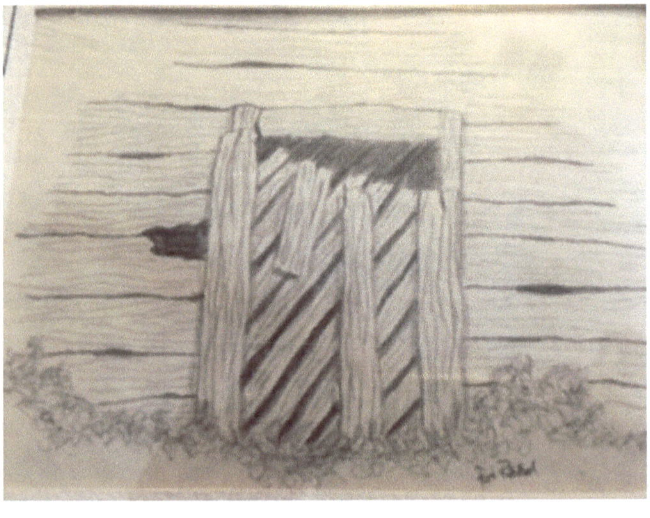

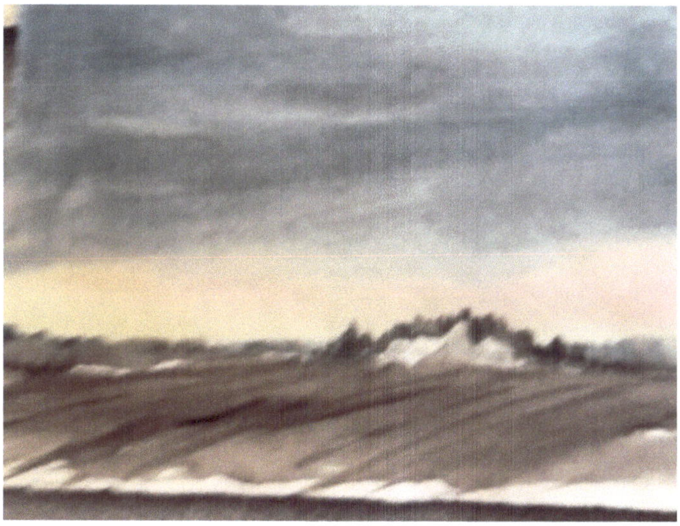

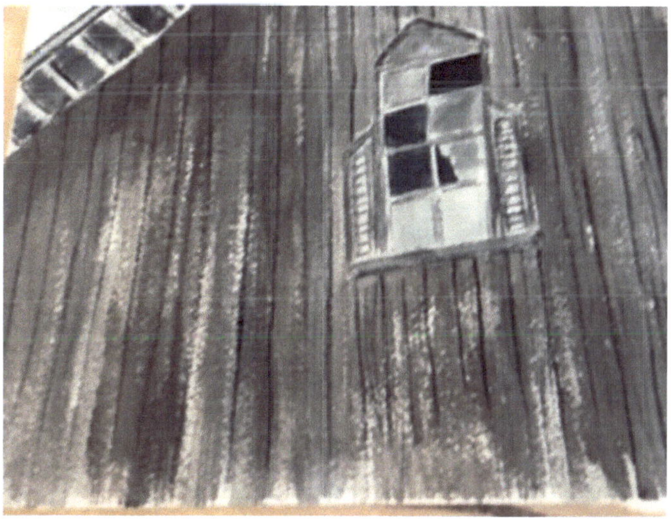

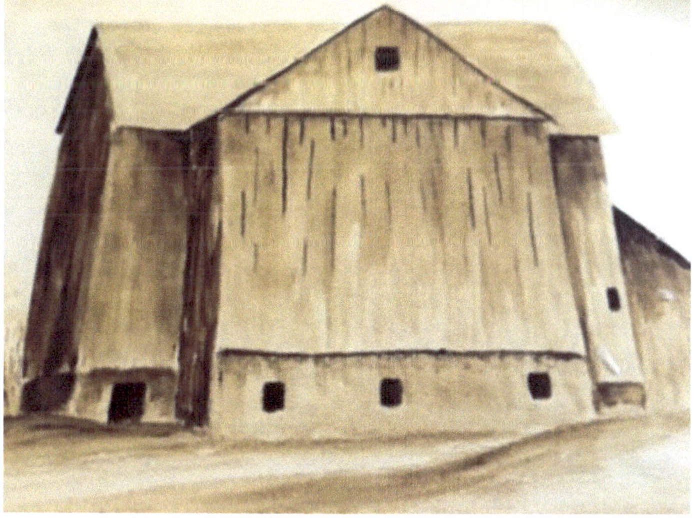

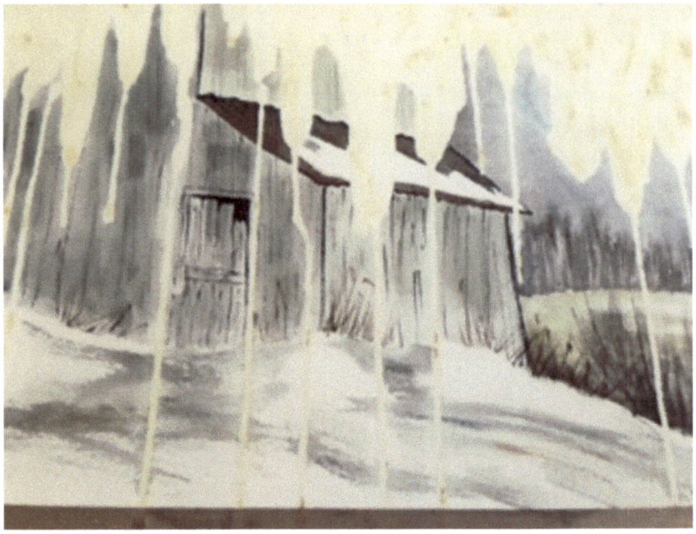

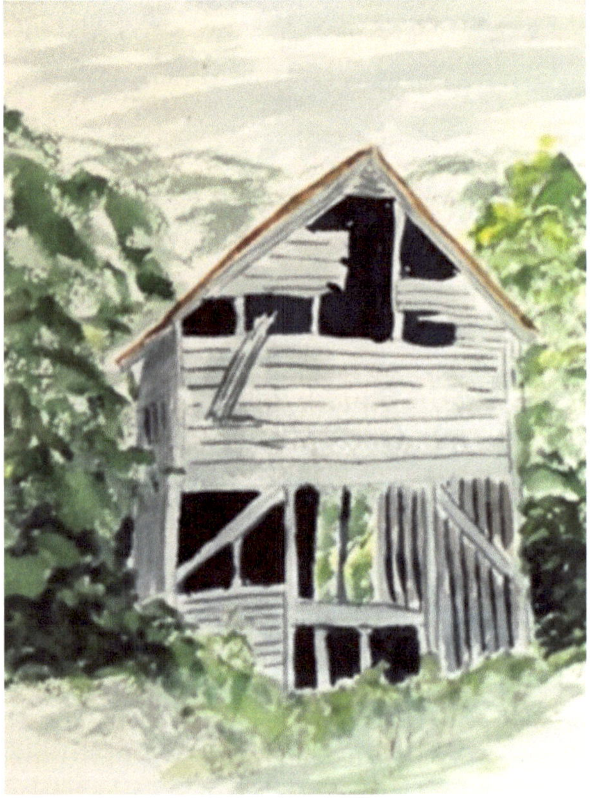

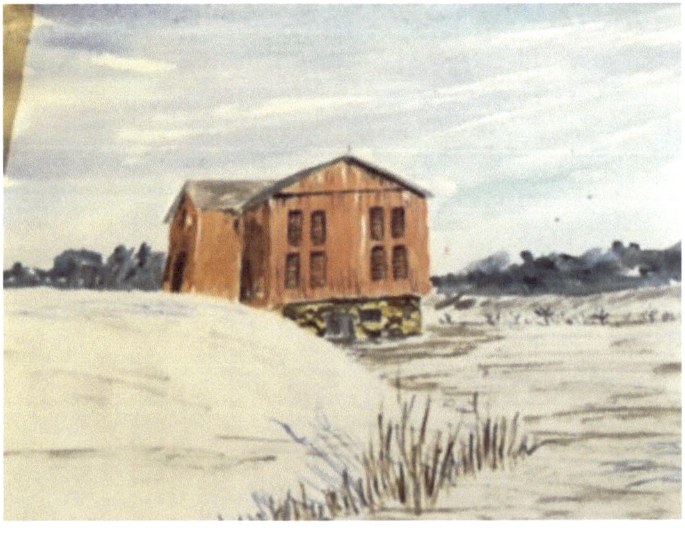

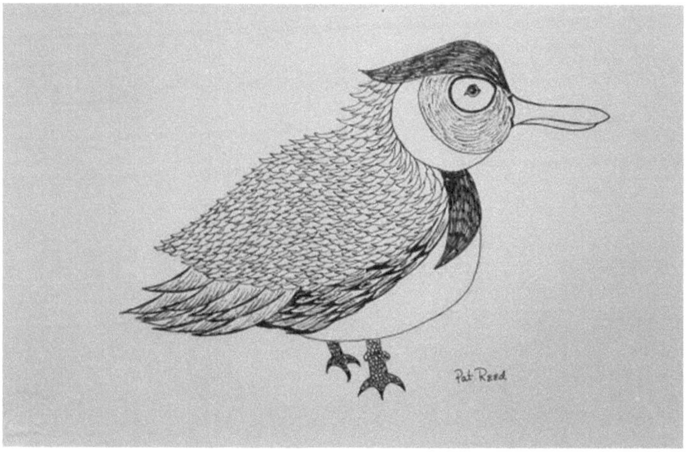
Pat Reed

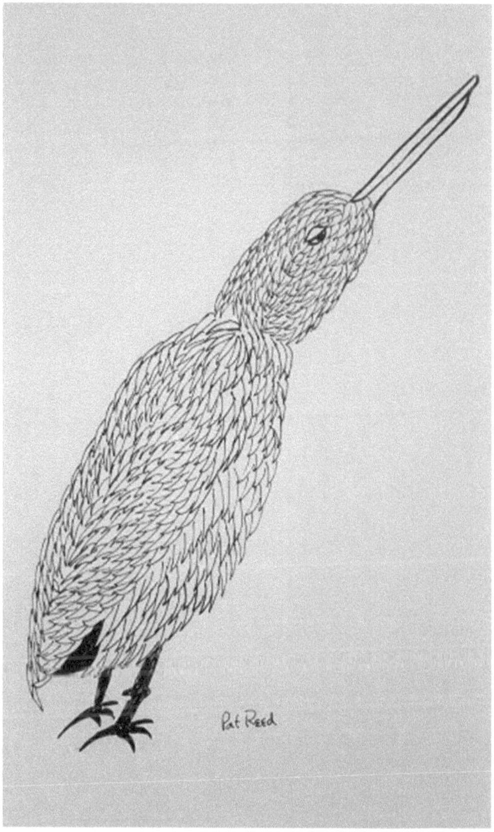
Pat Reed

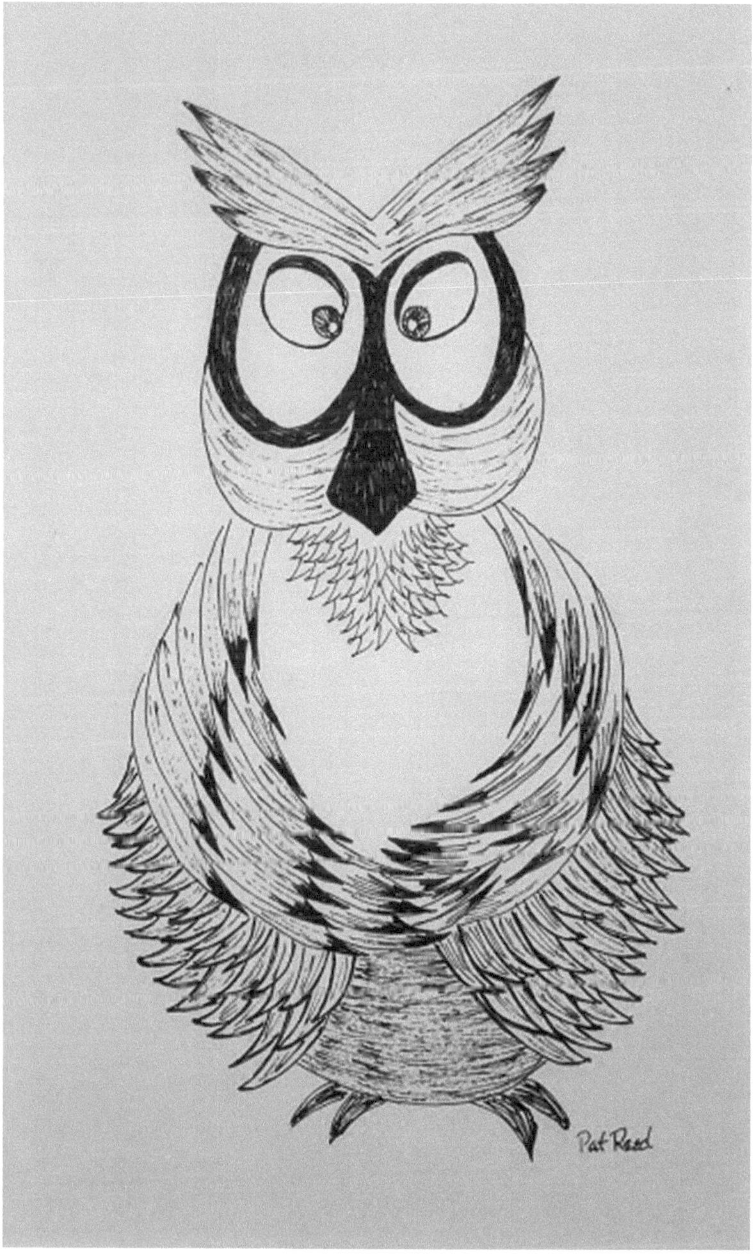
Pat Reed

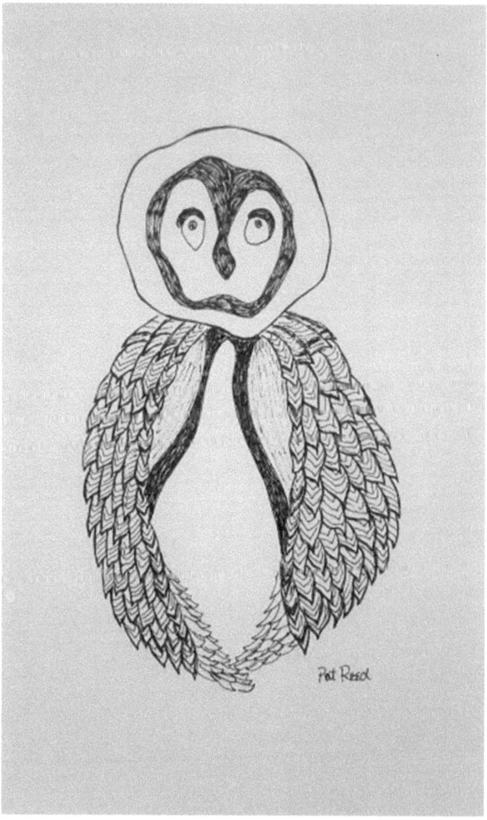
Pat Reed

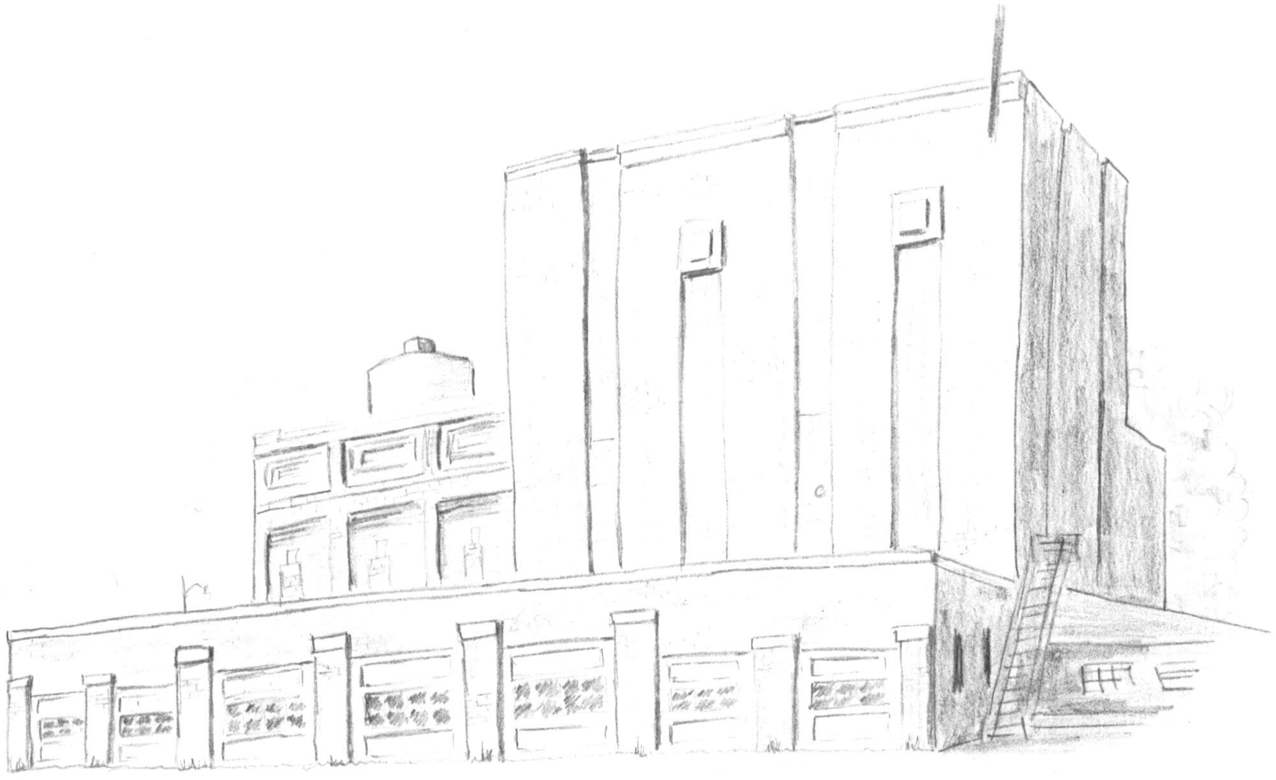

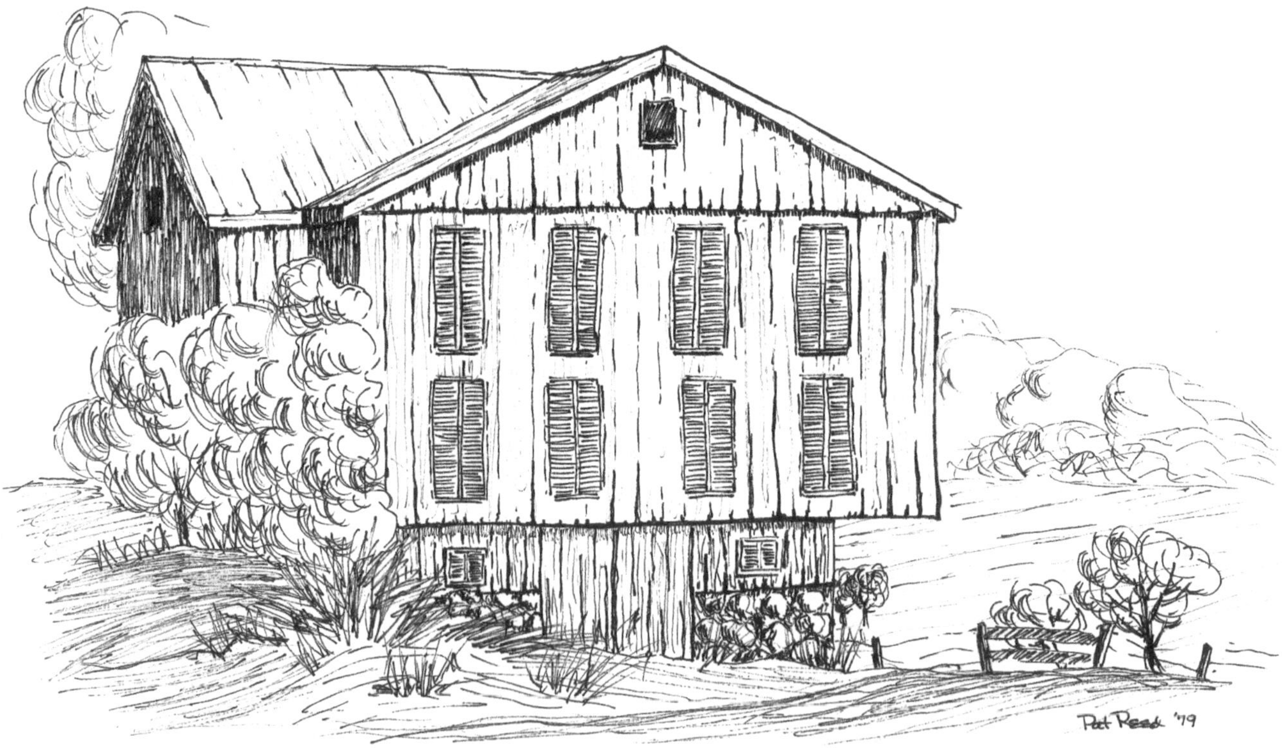
Pat Reed '79

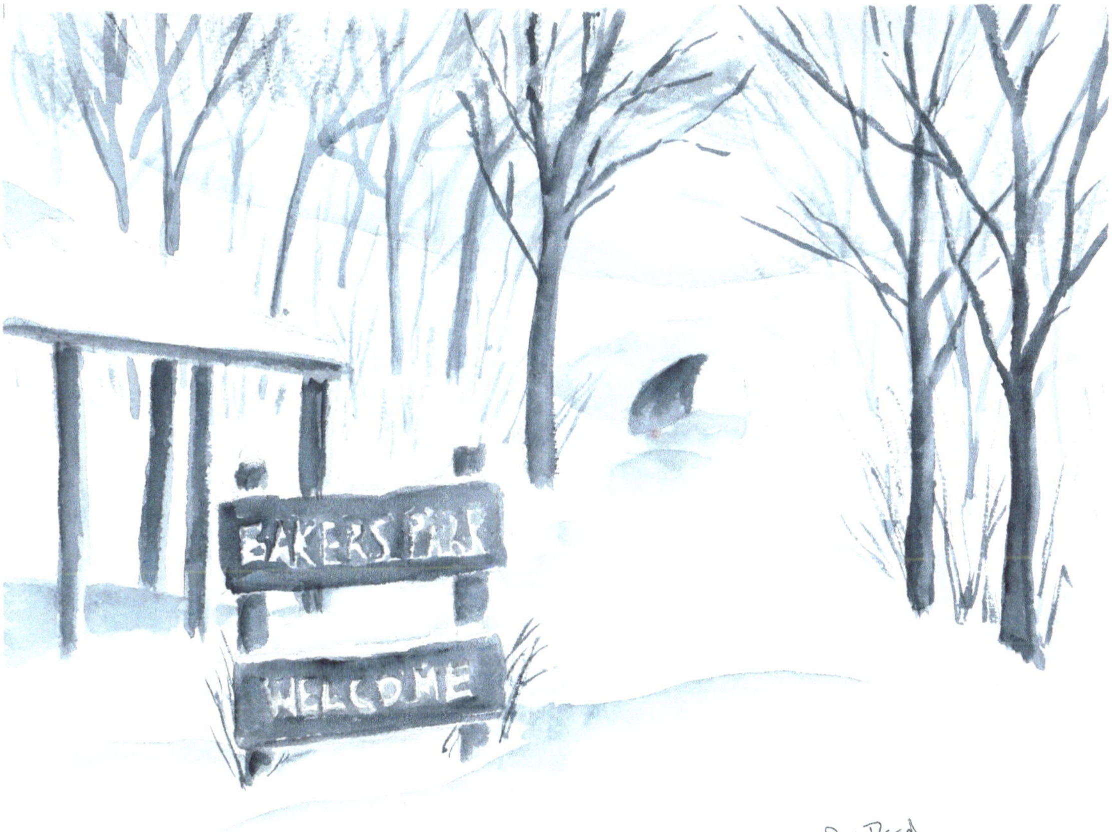

Pat Reed

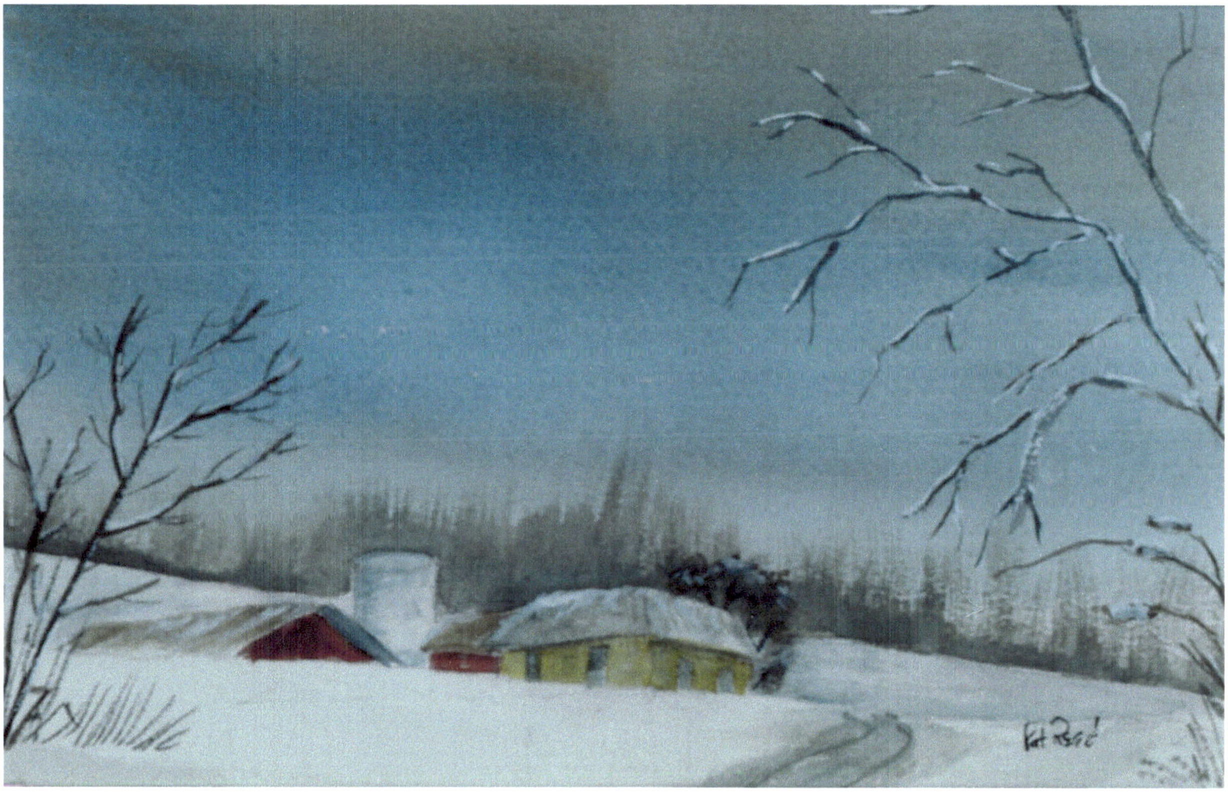

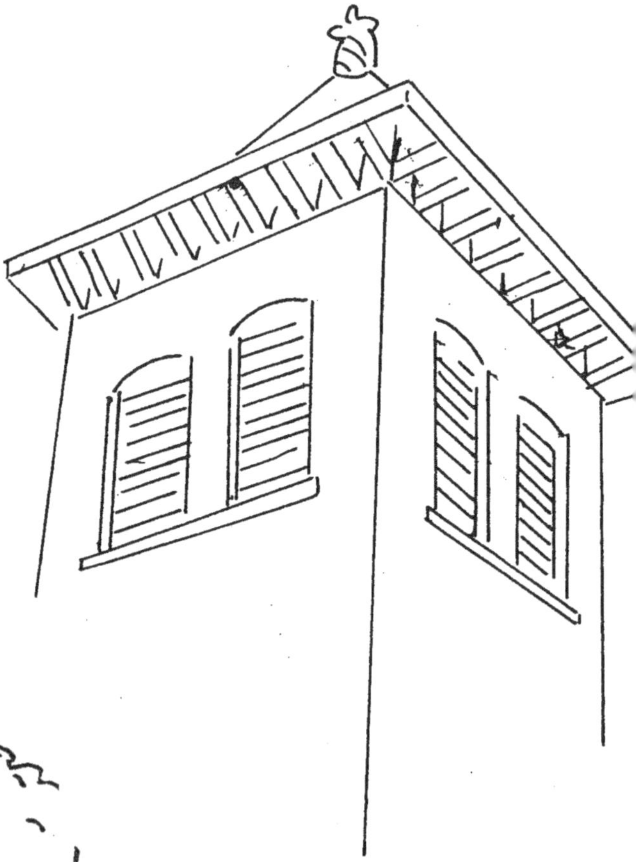

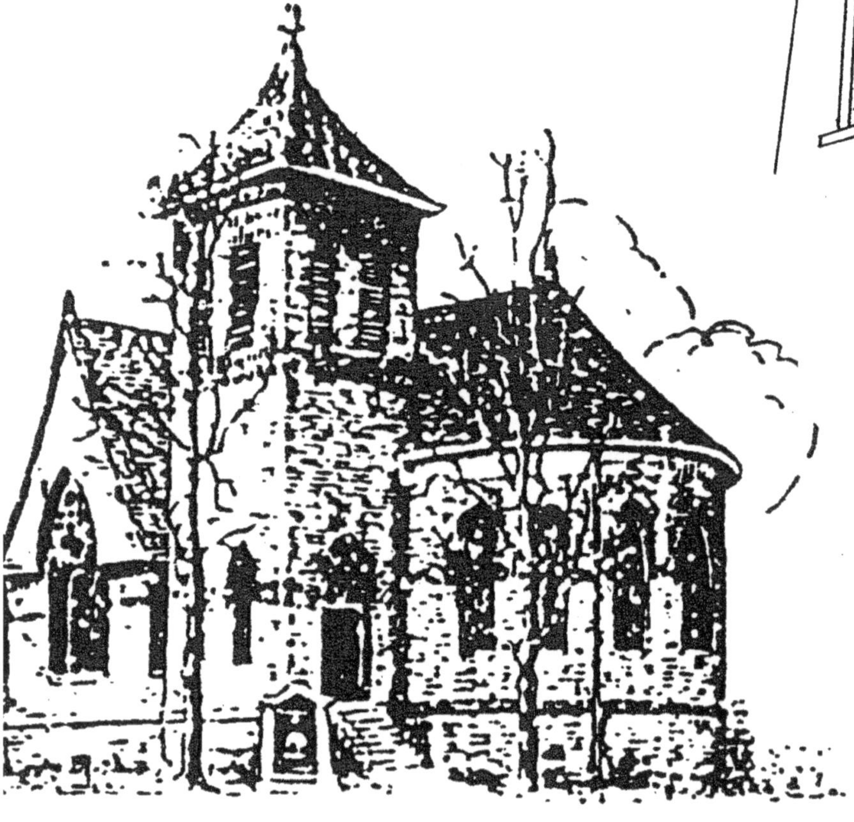

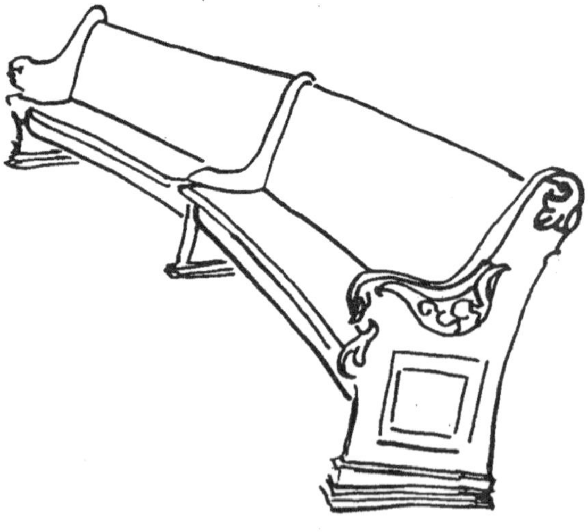

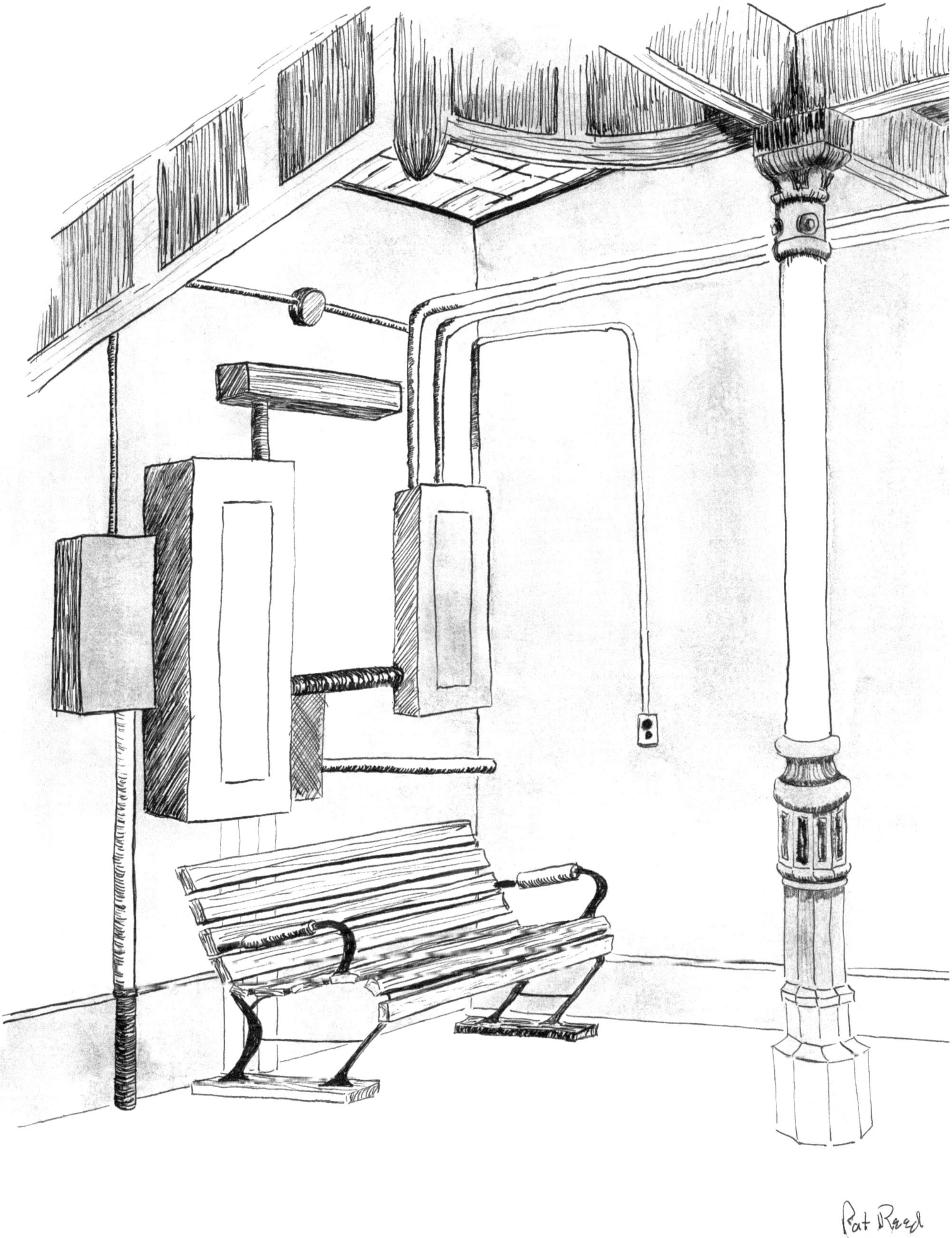
Pat Reed

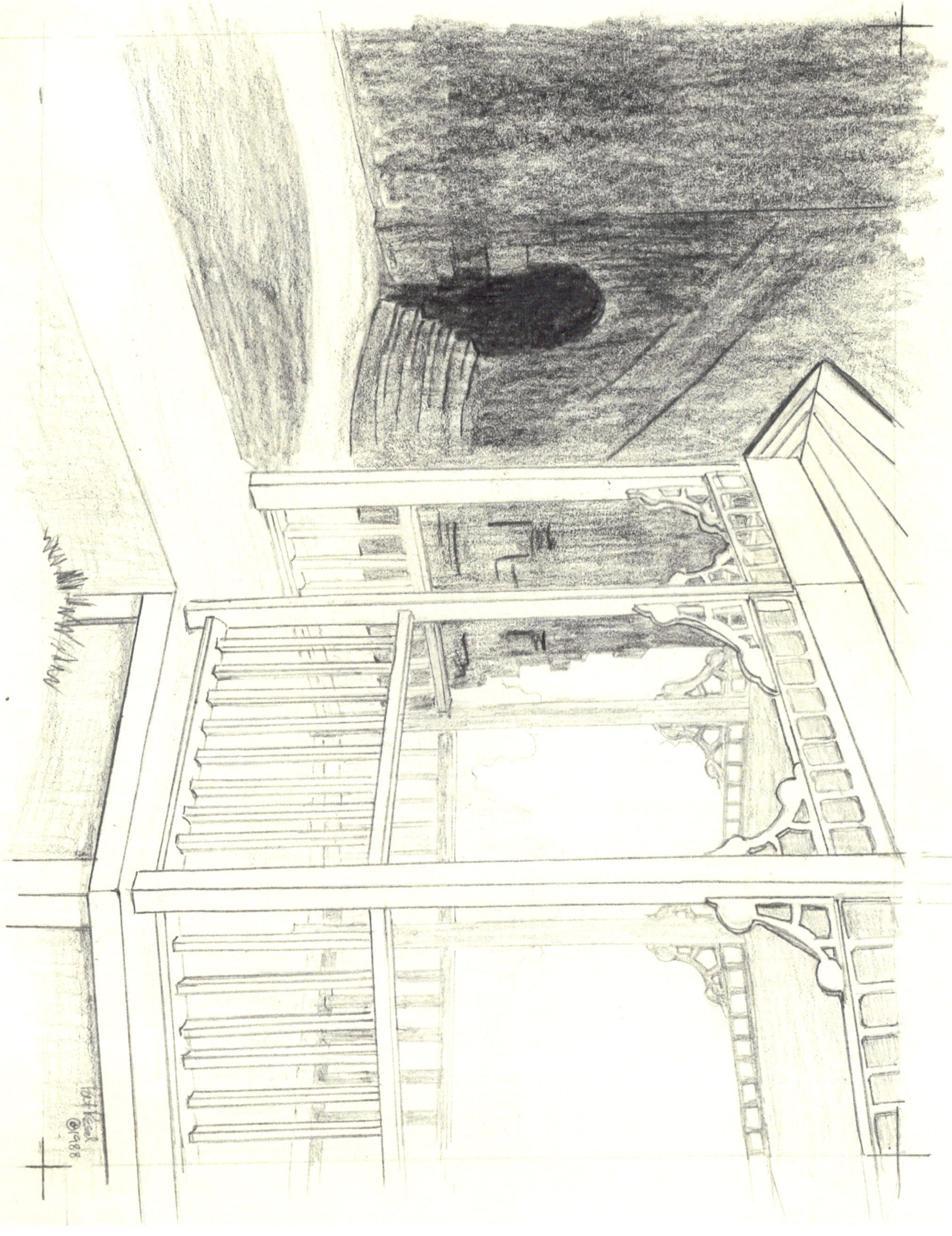
©1988

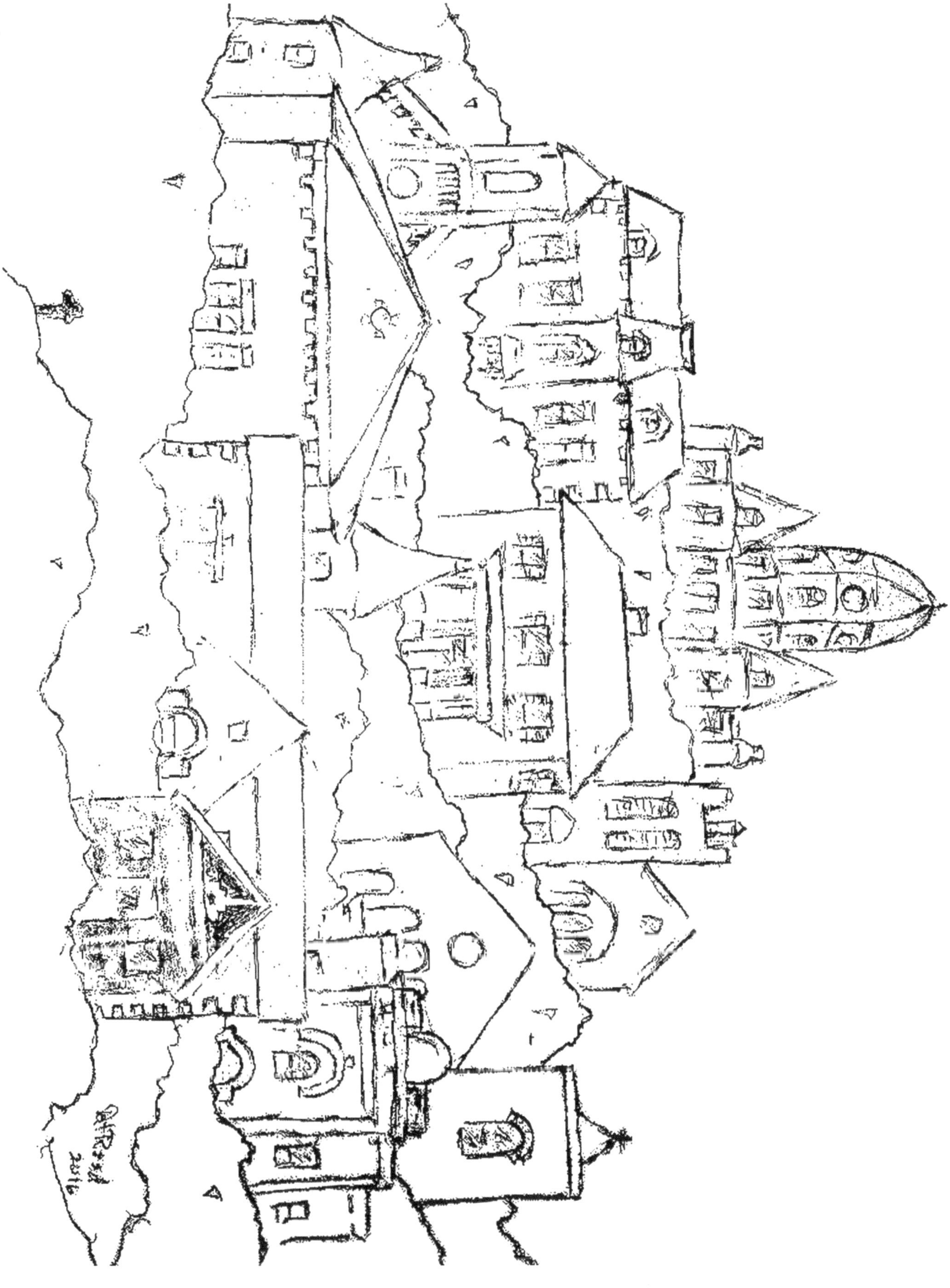

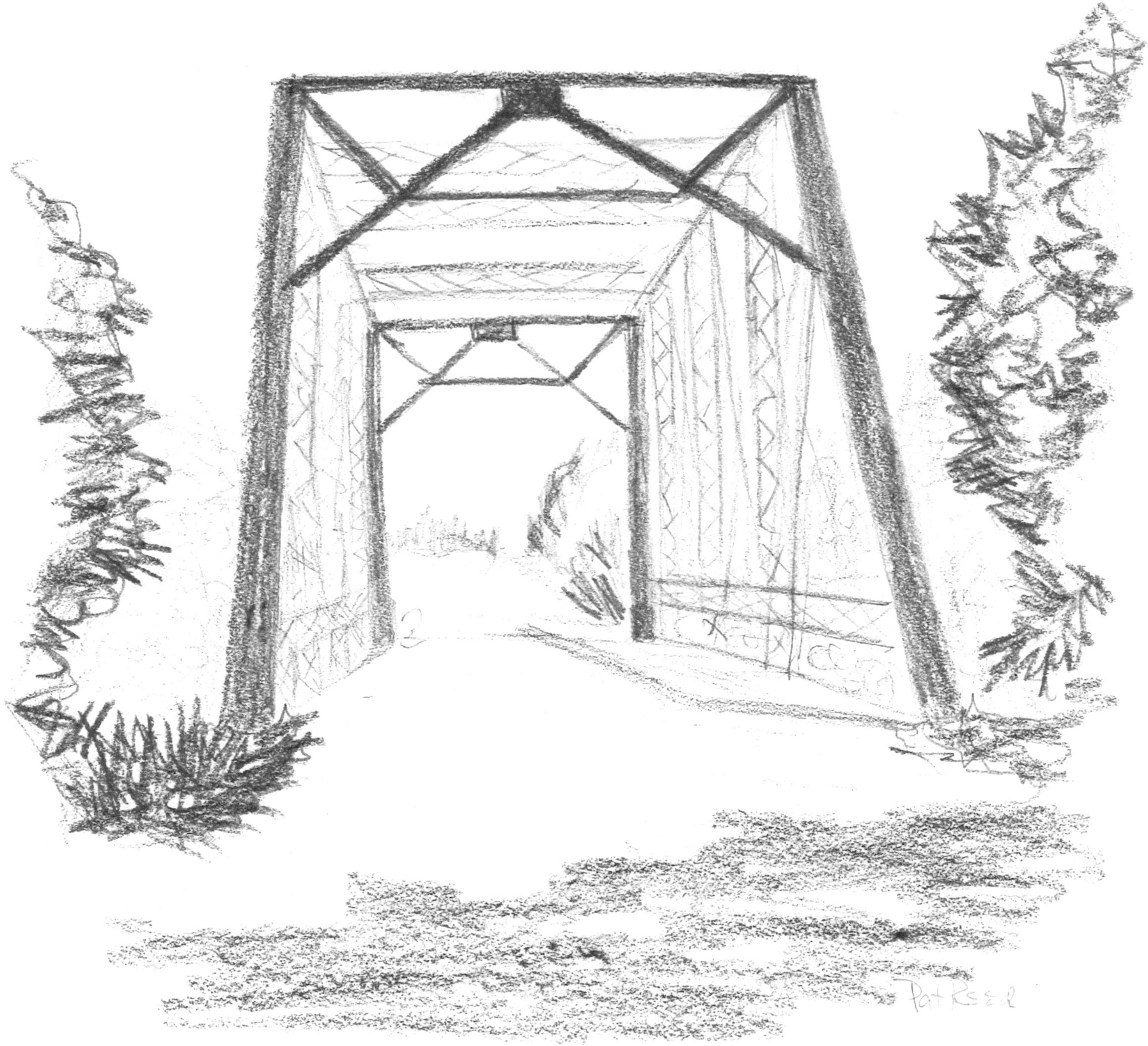
Pat Reed

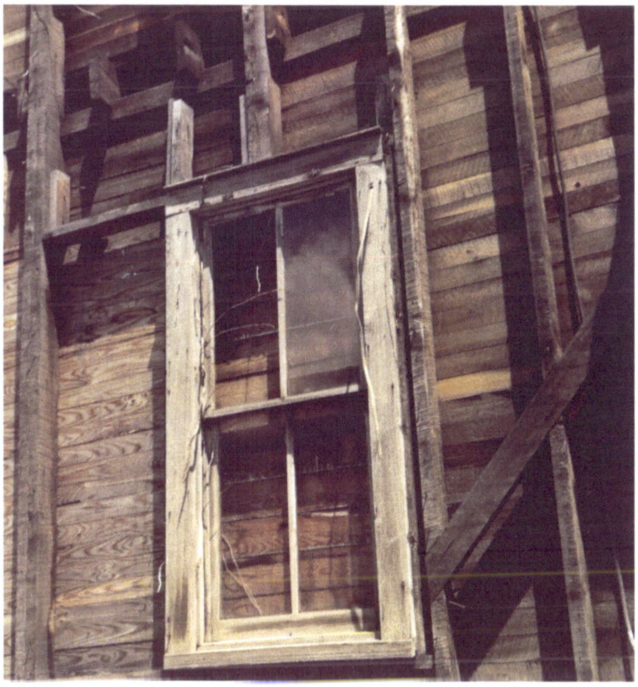

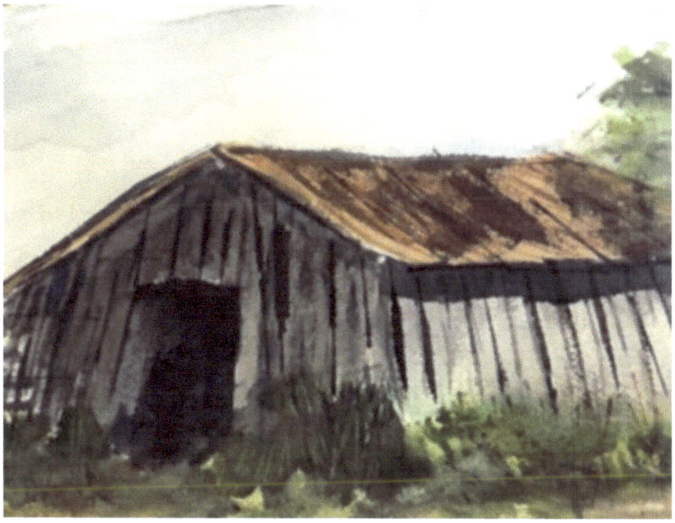

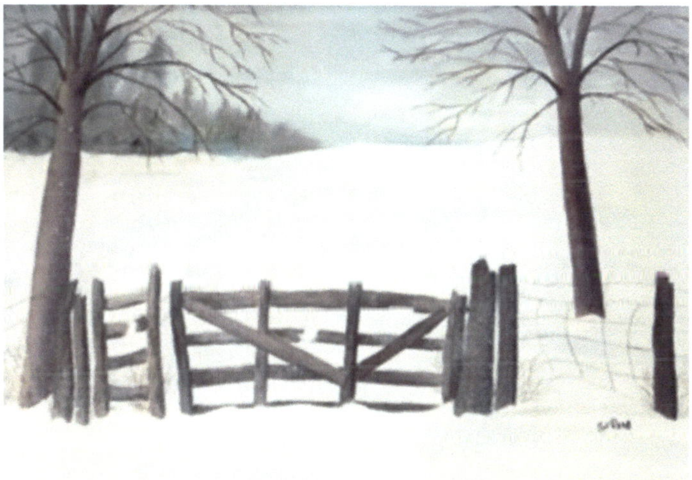

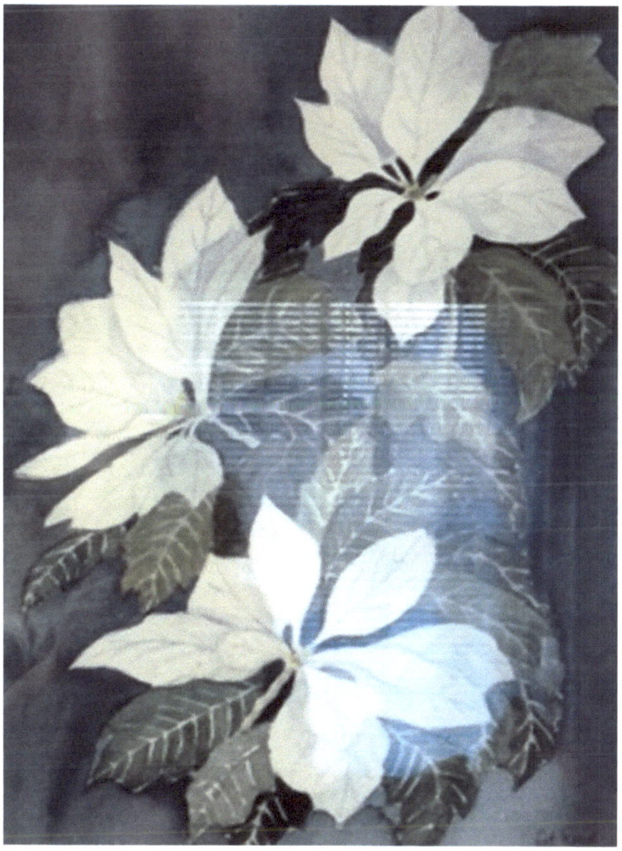

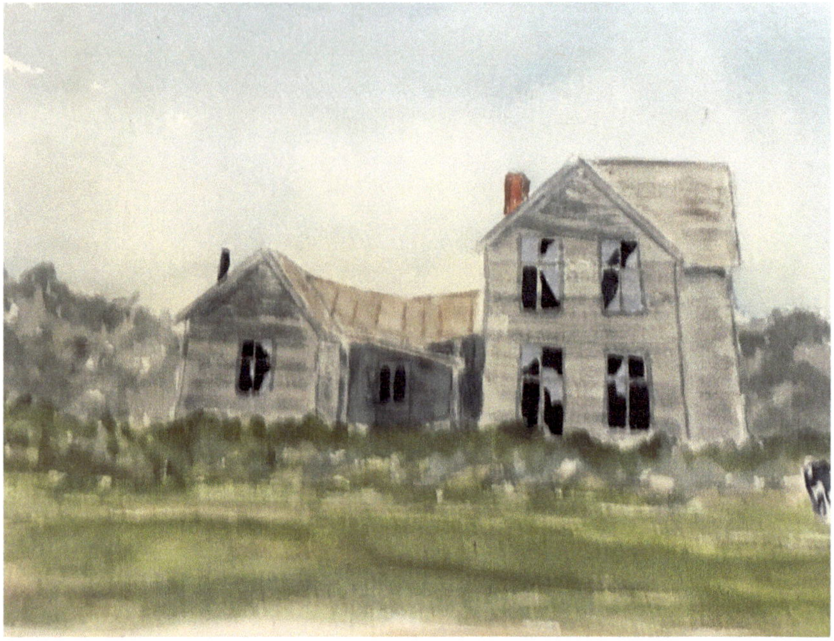

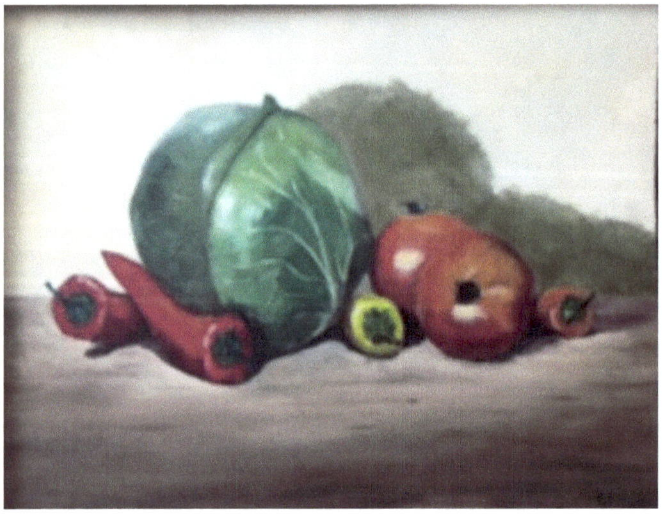

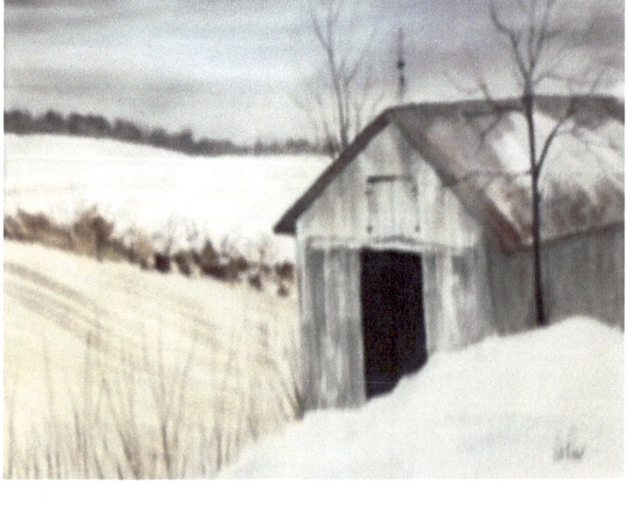

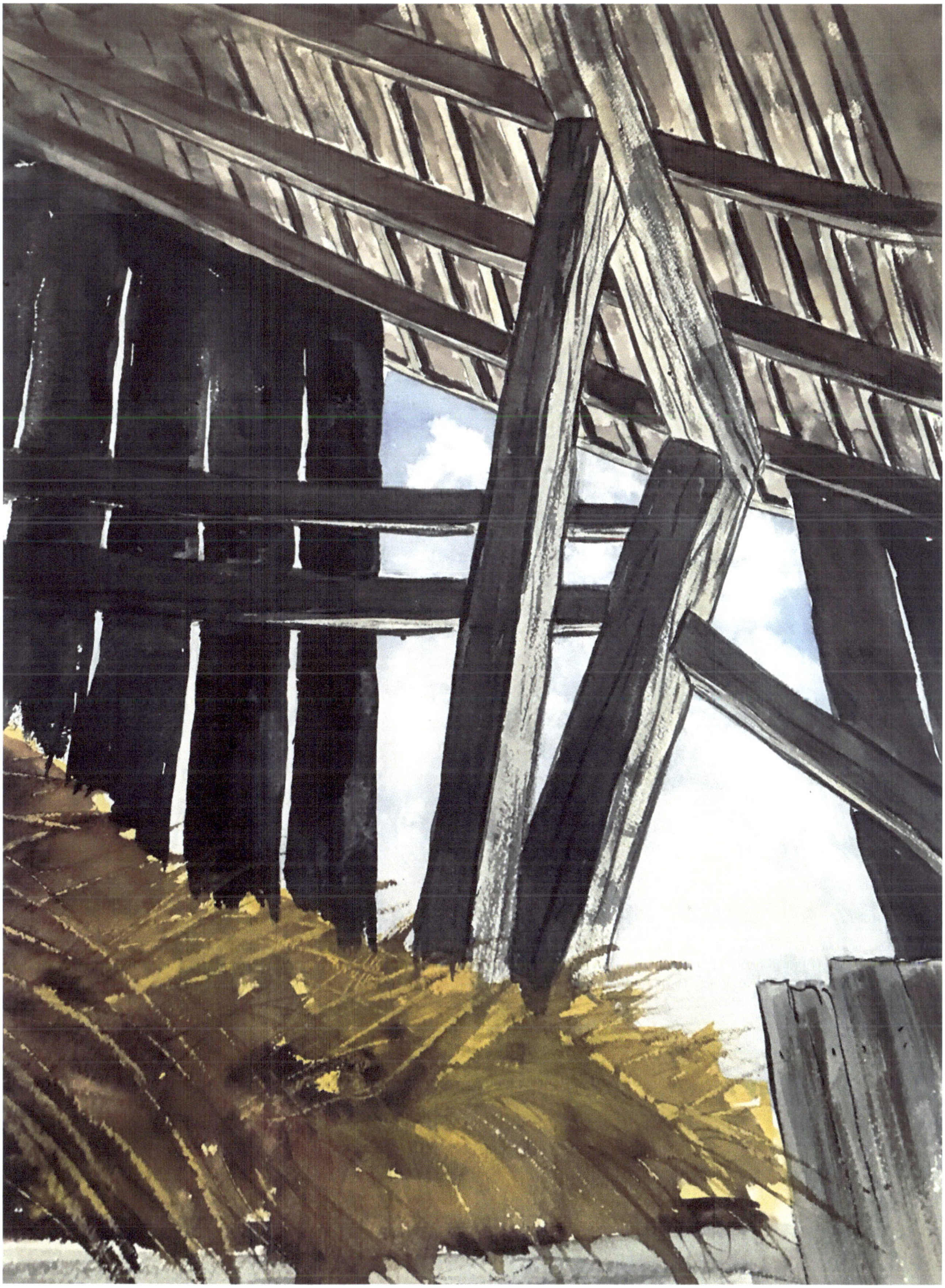

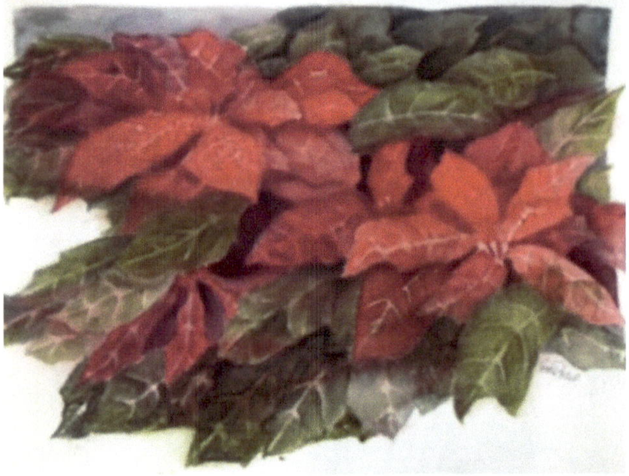

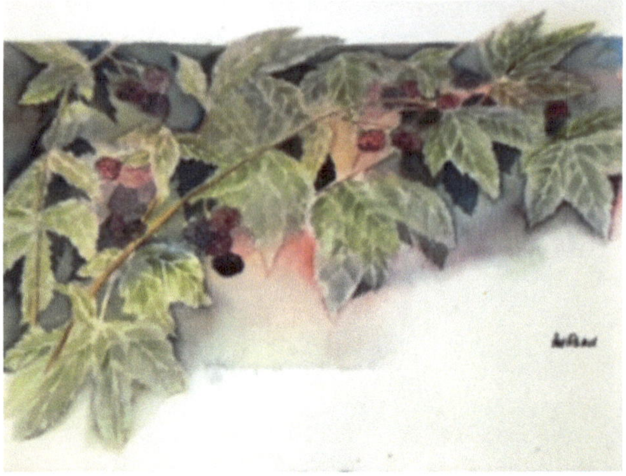

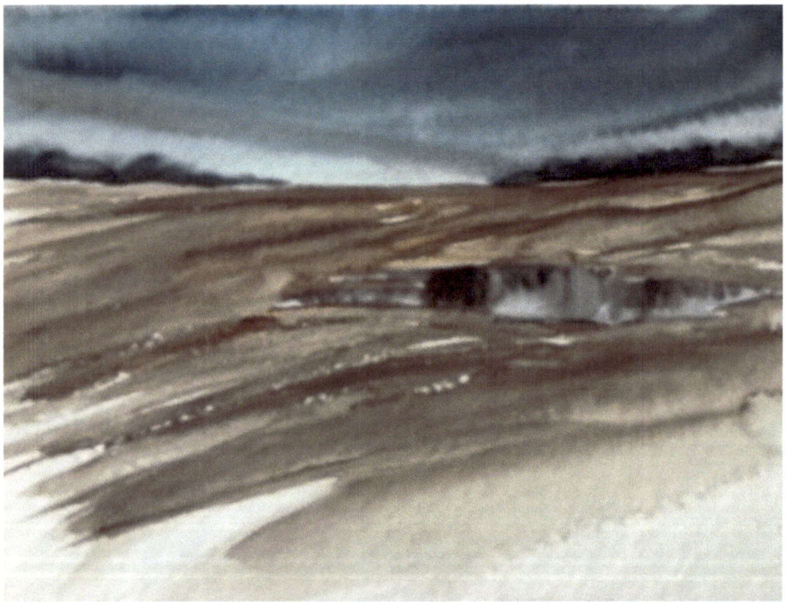

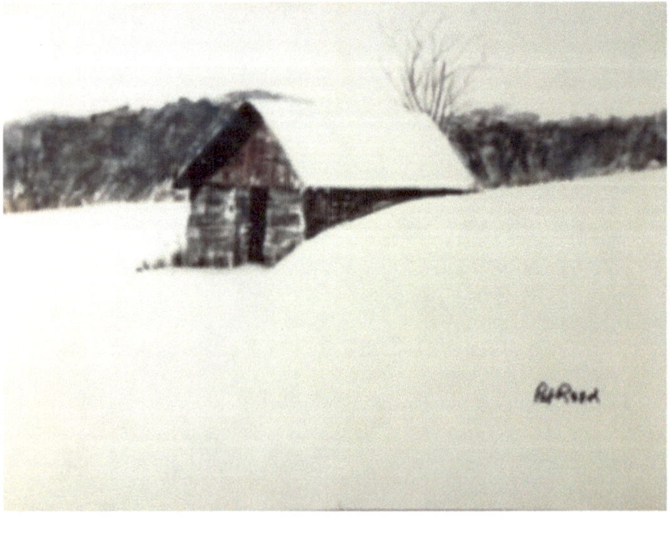

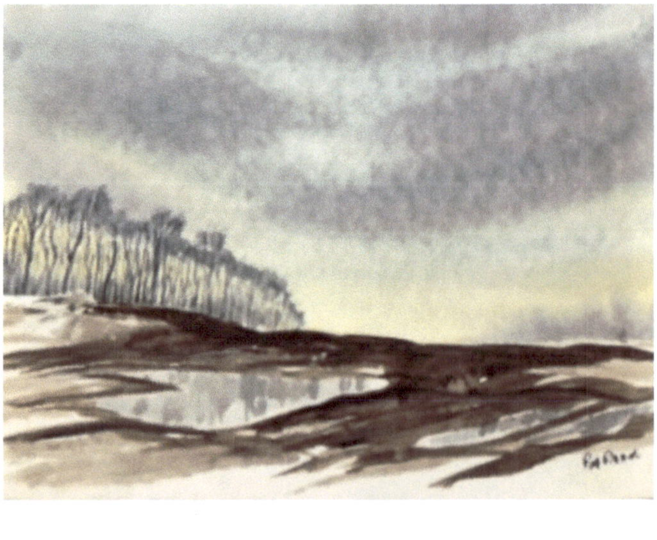

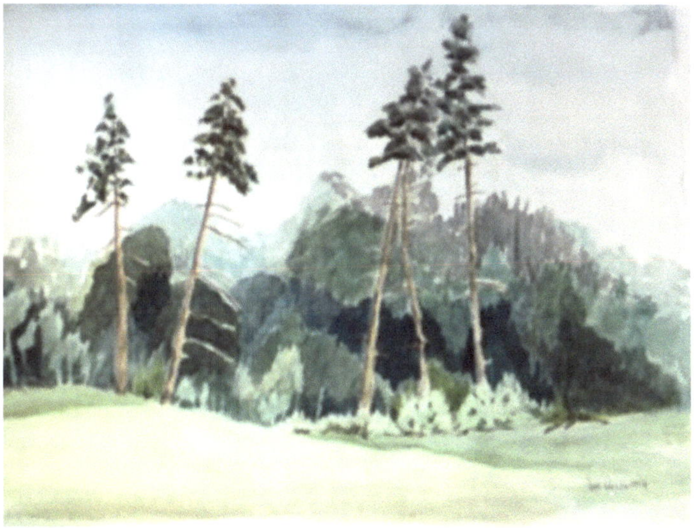

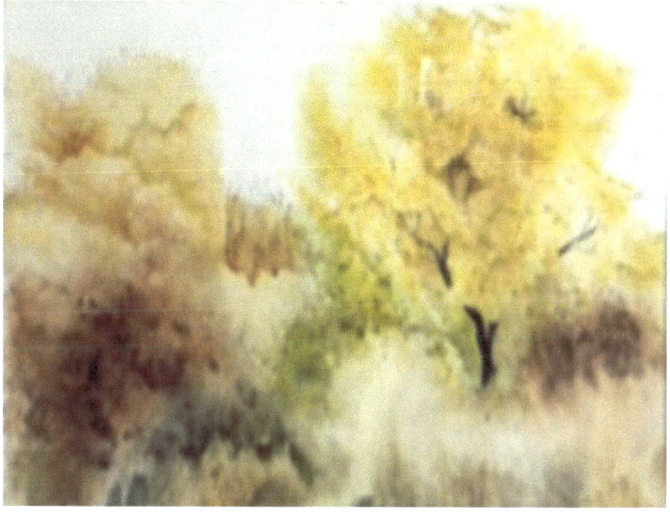

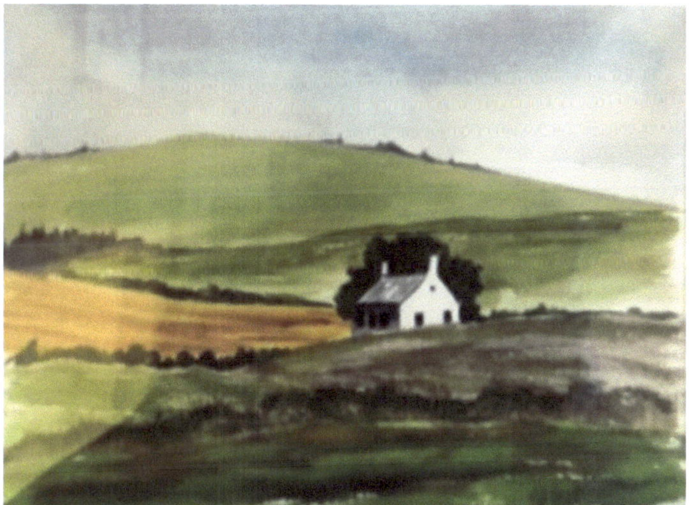

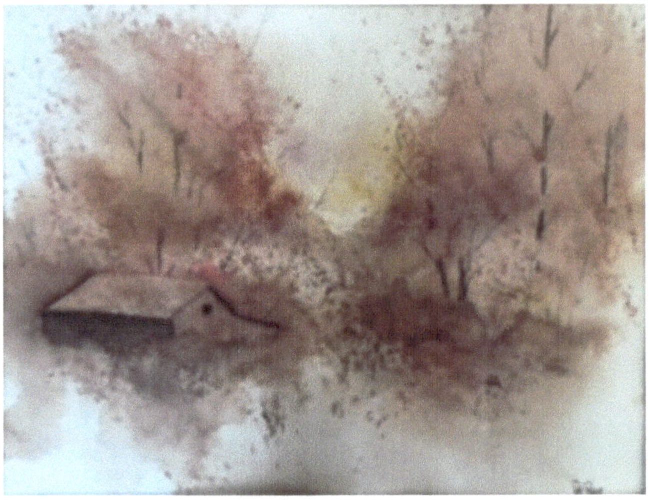

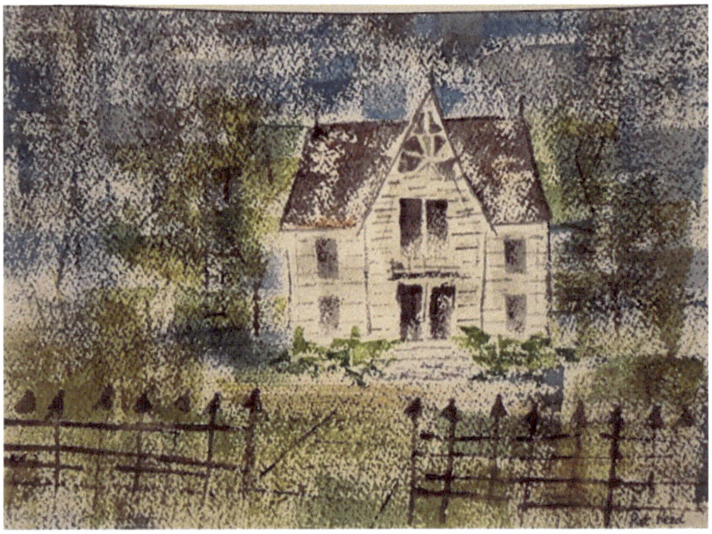

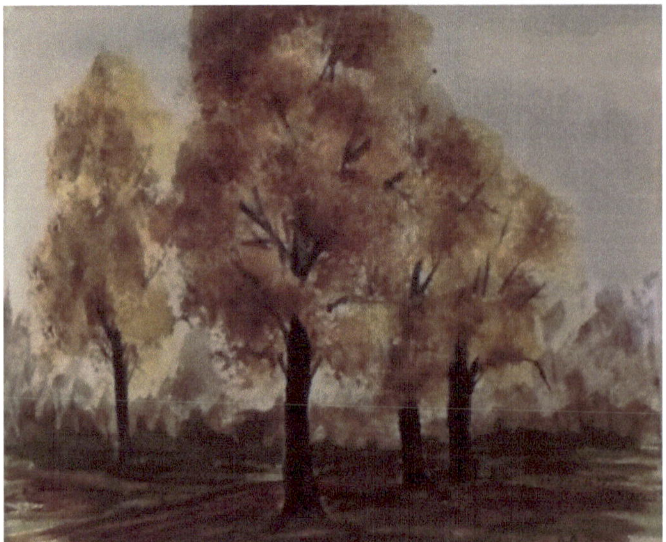

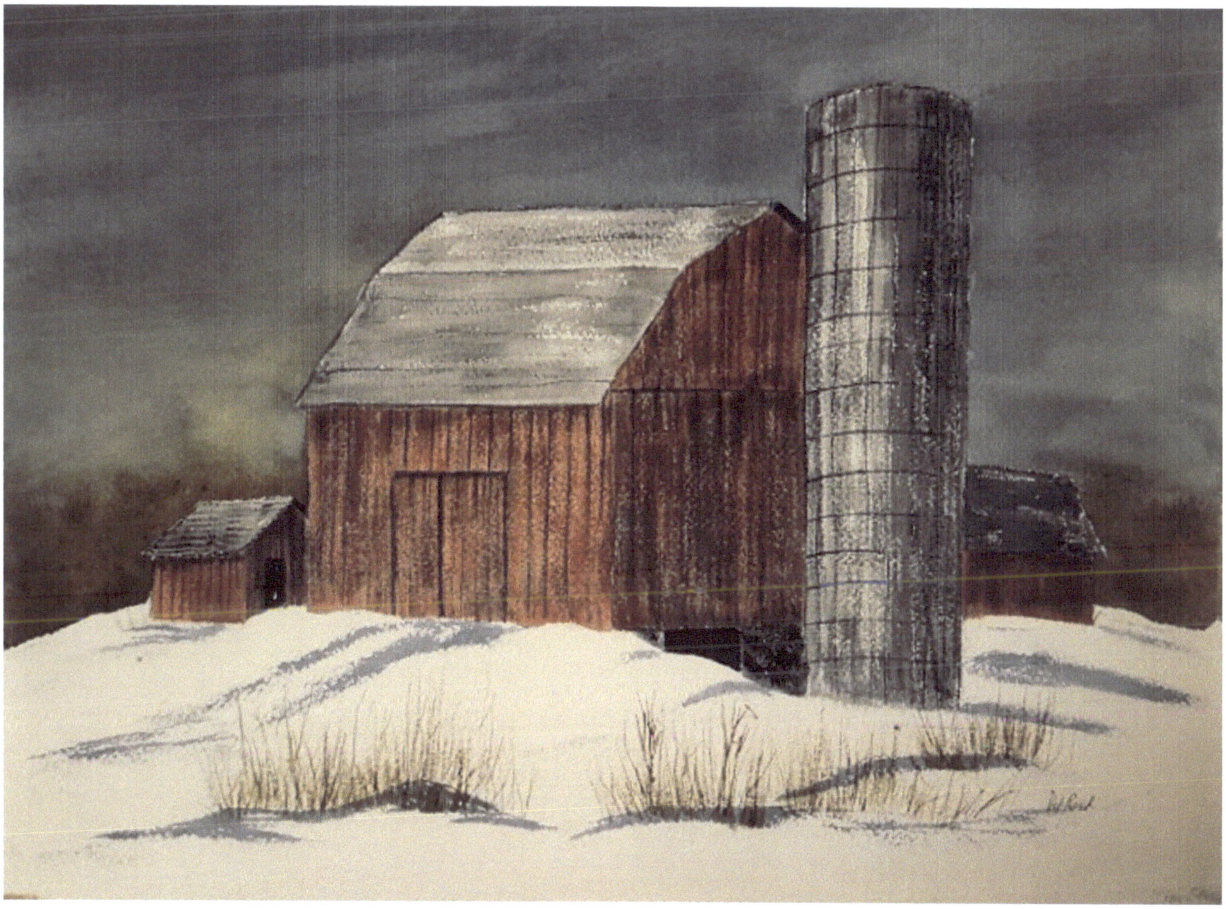

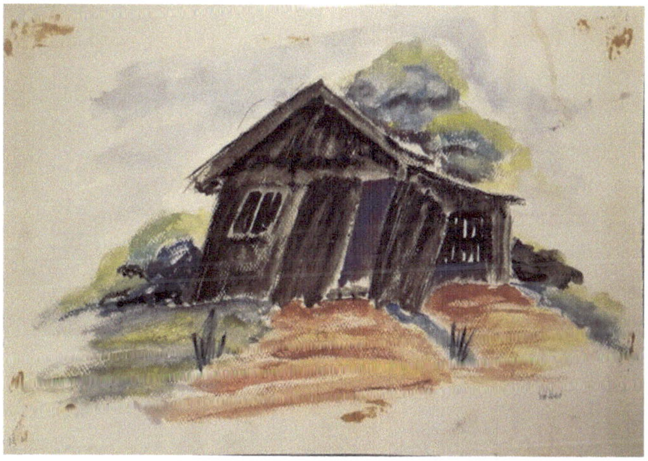

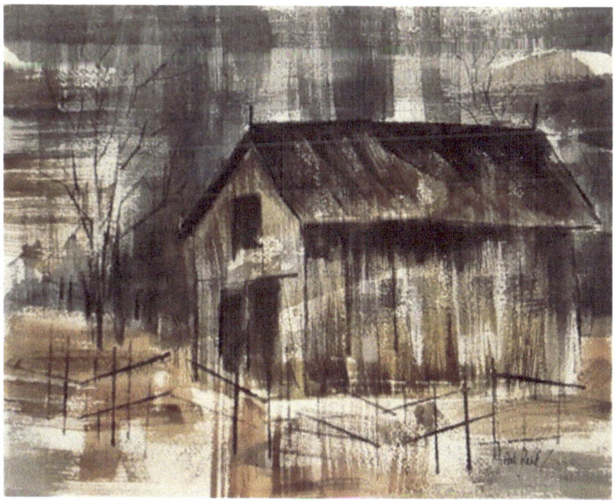

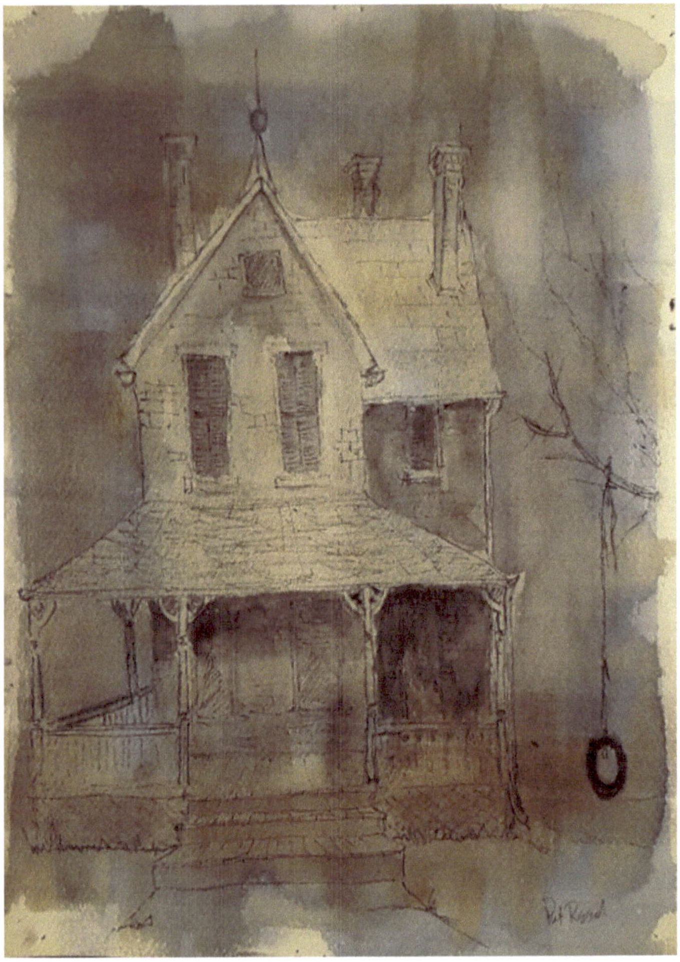

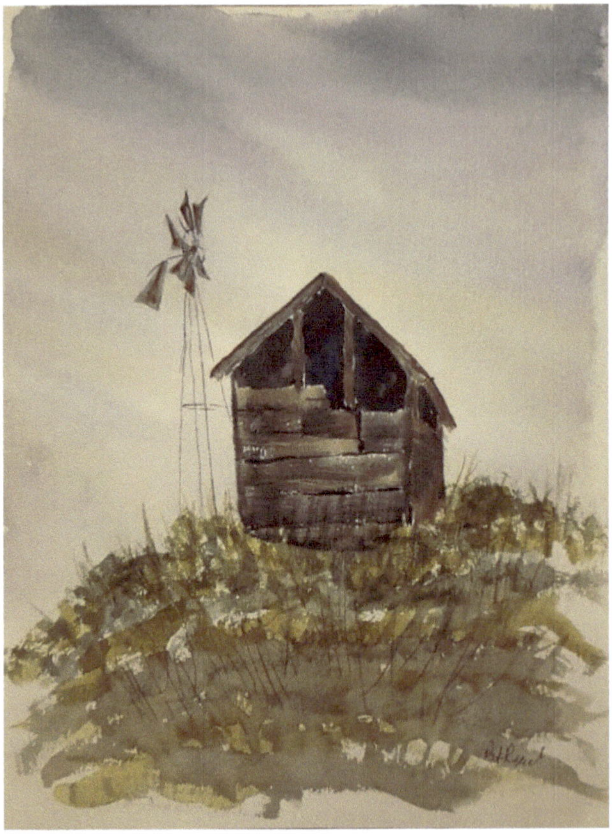

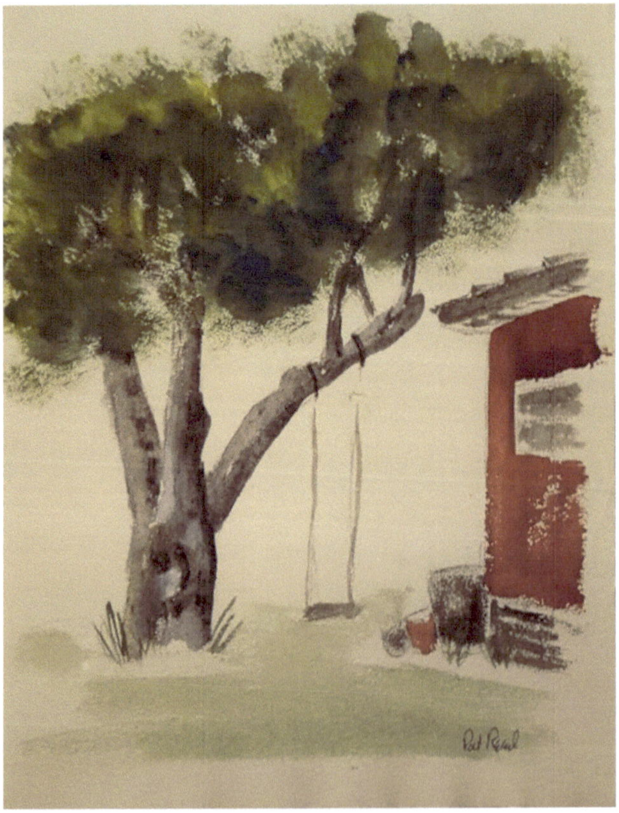

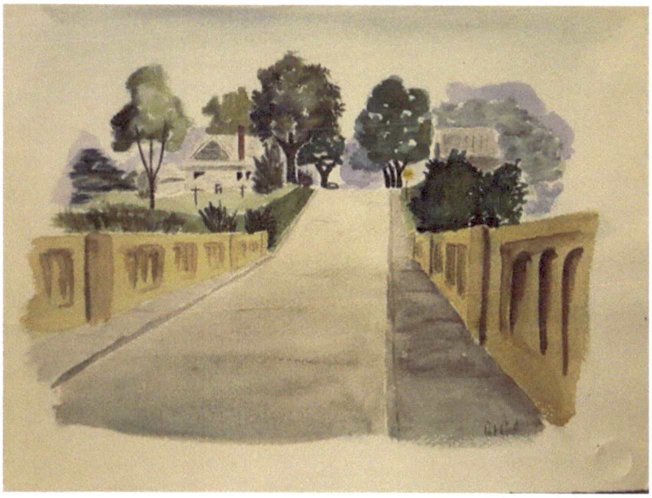

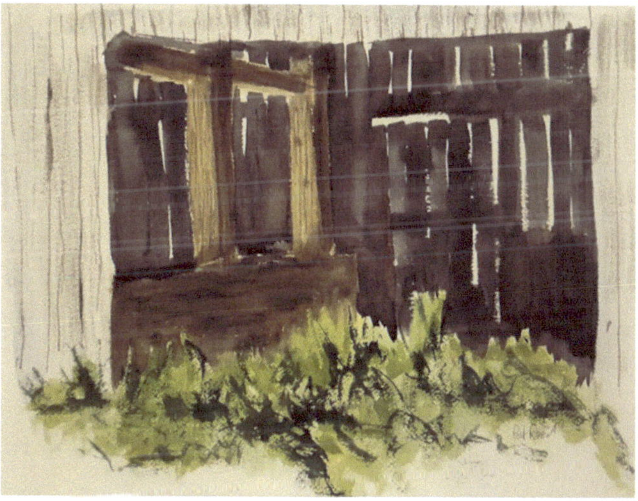

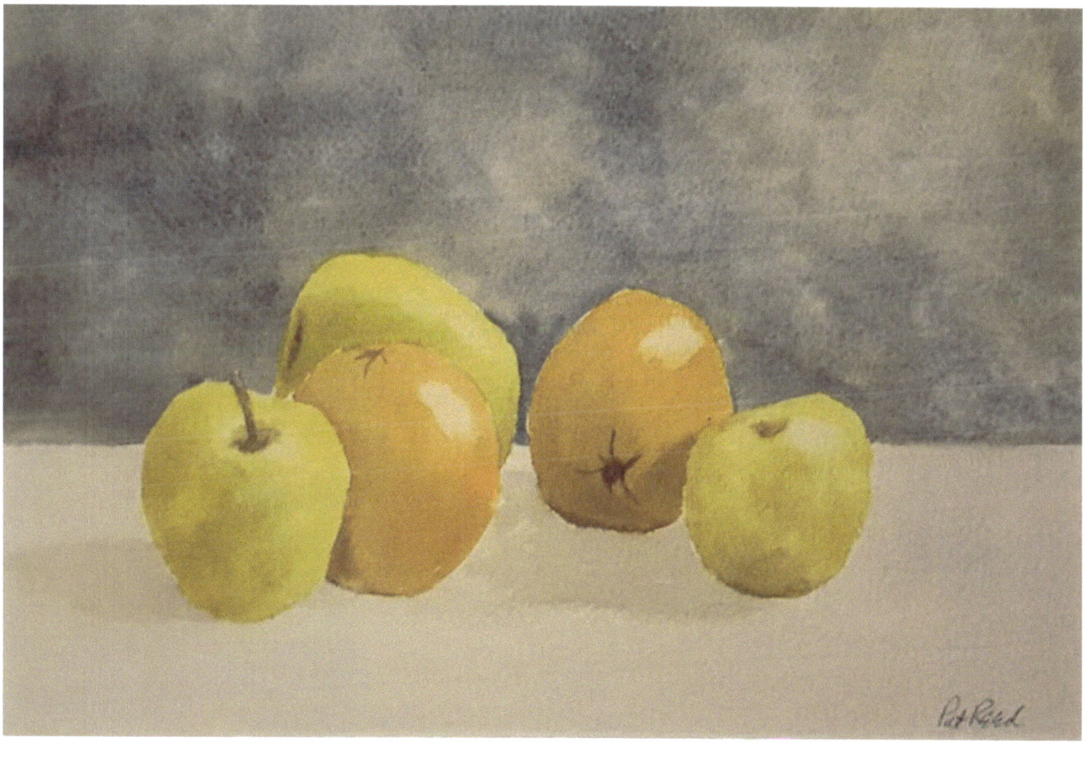

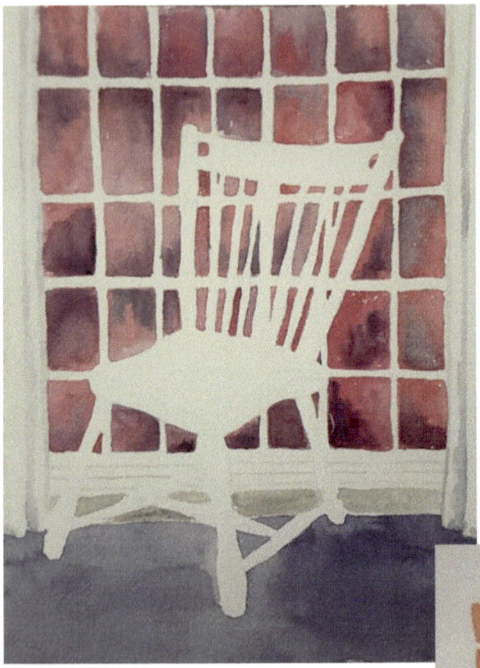

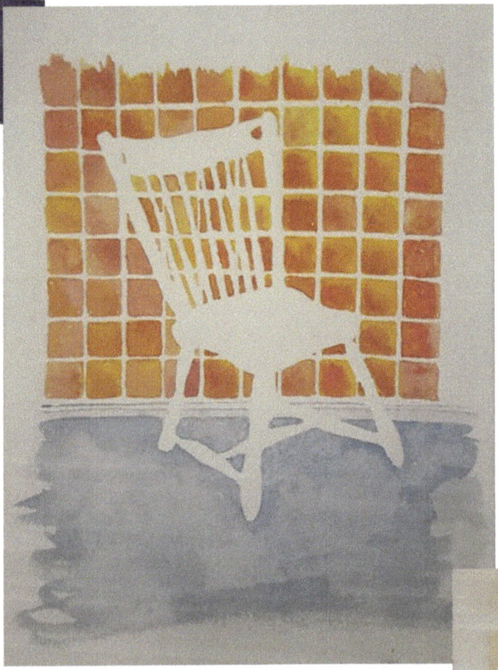

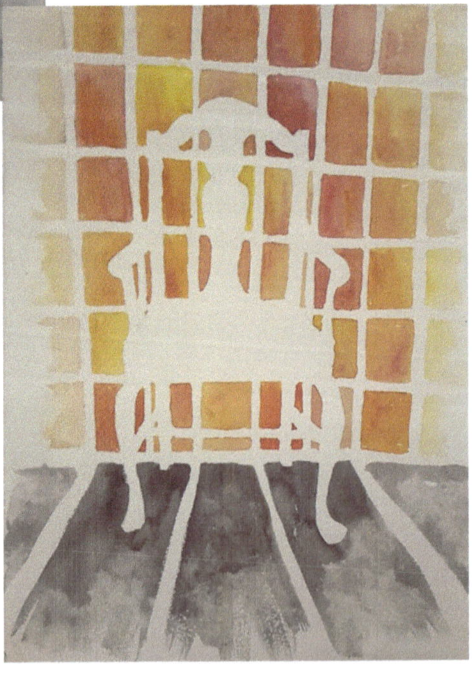

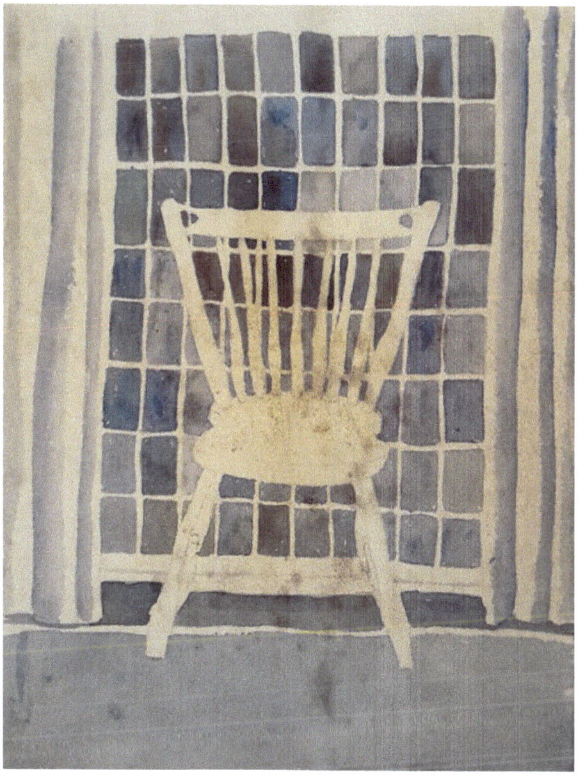

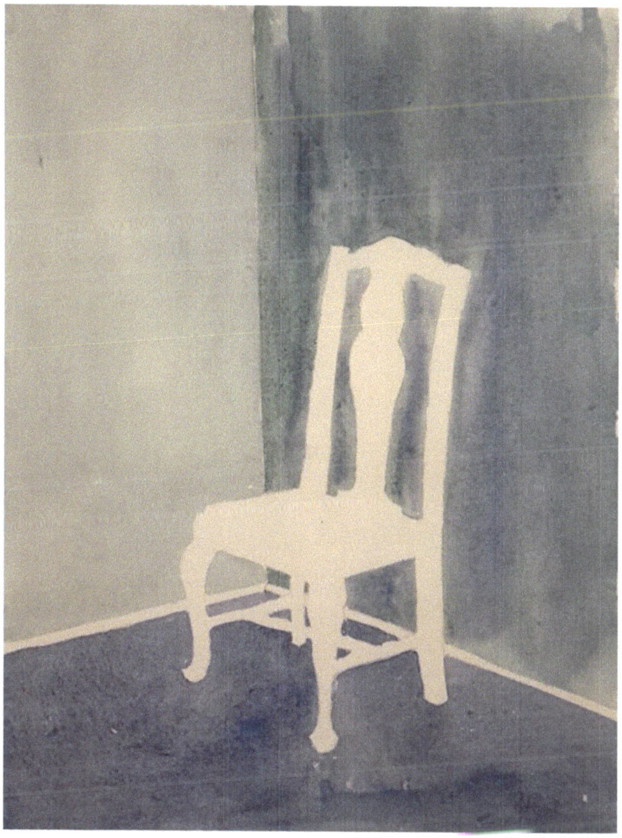

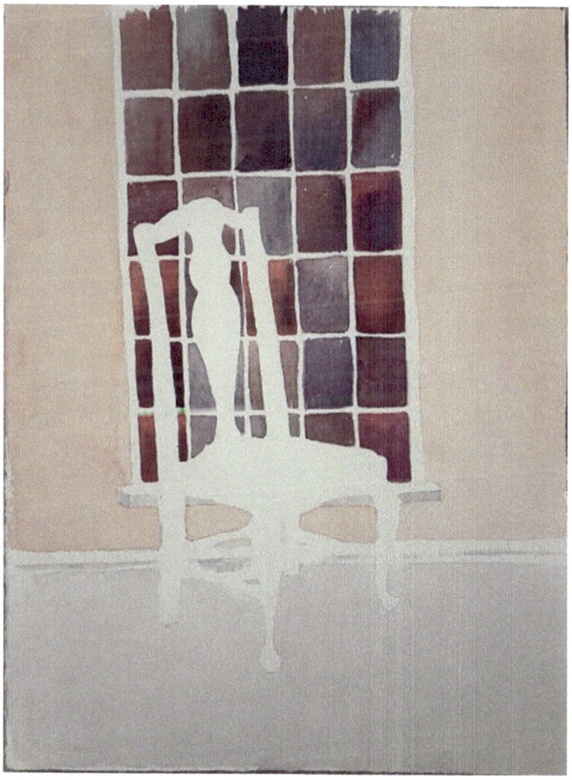

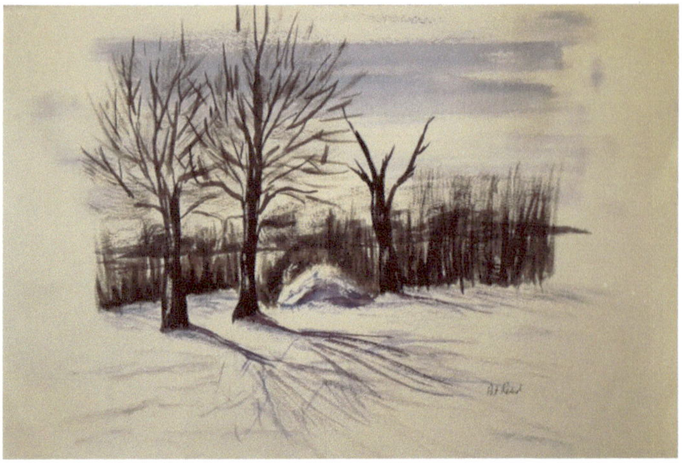

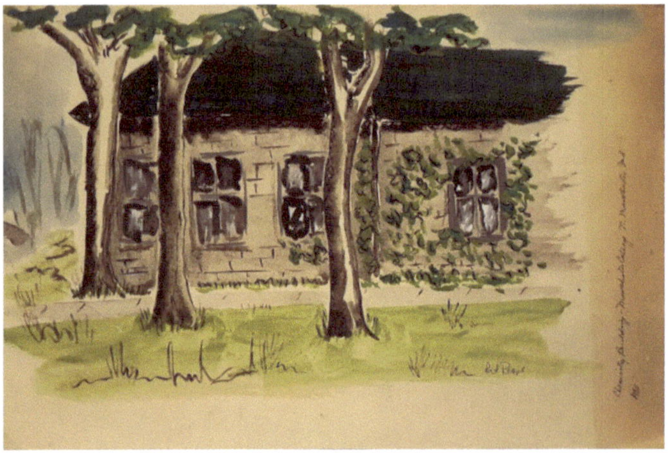

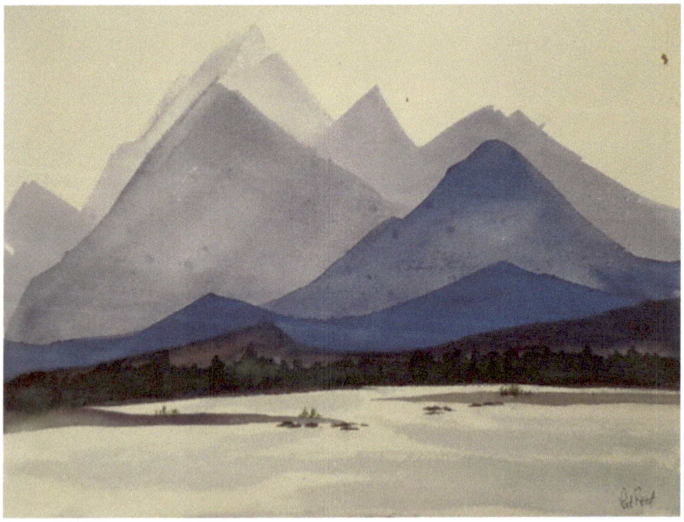

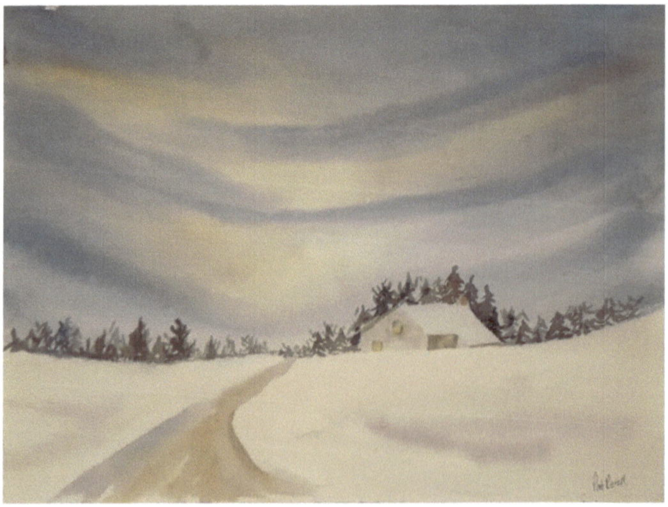

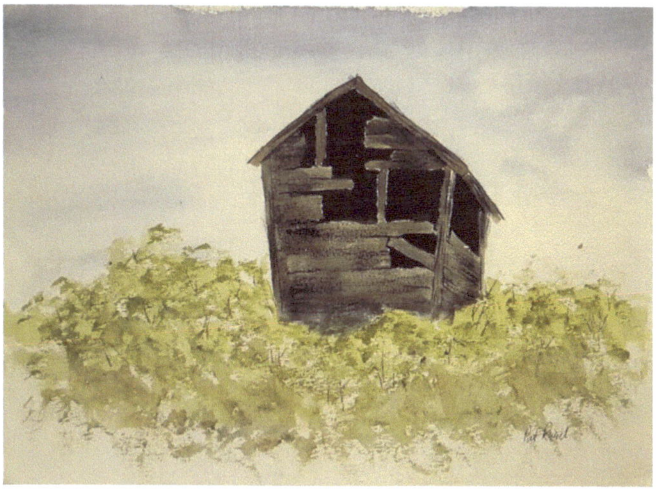

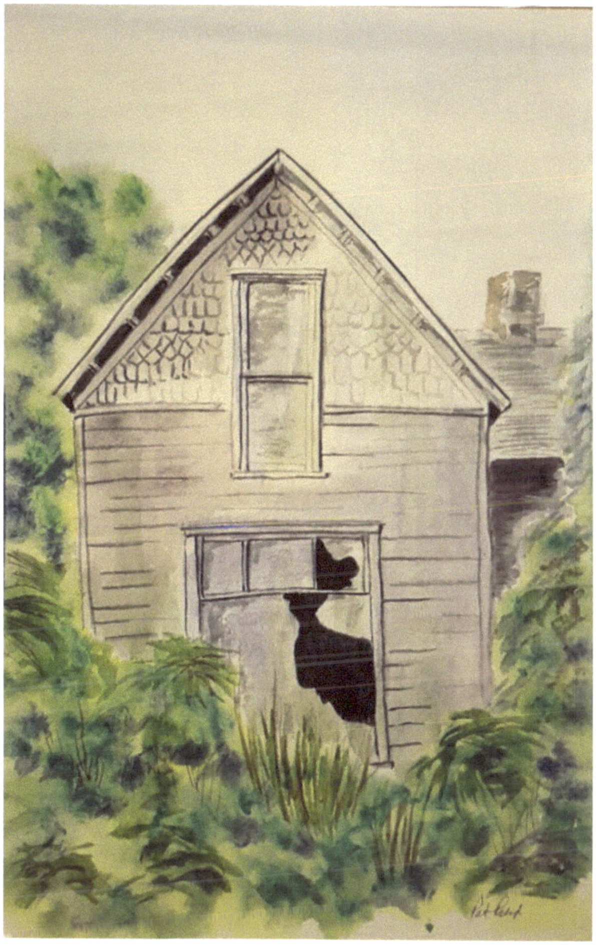

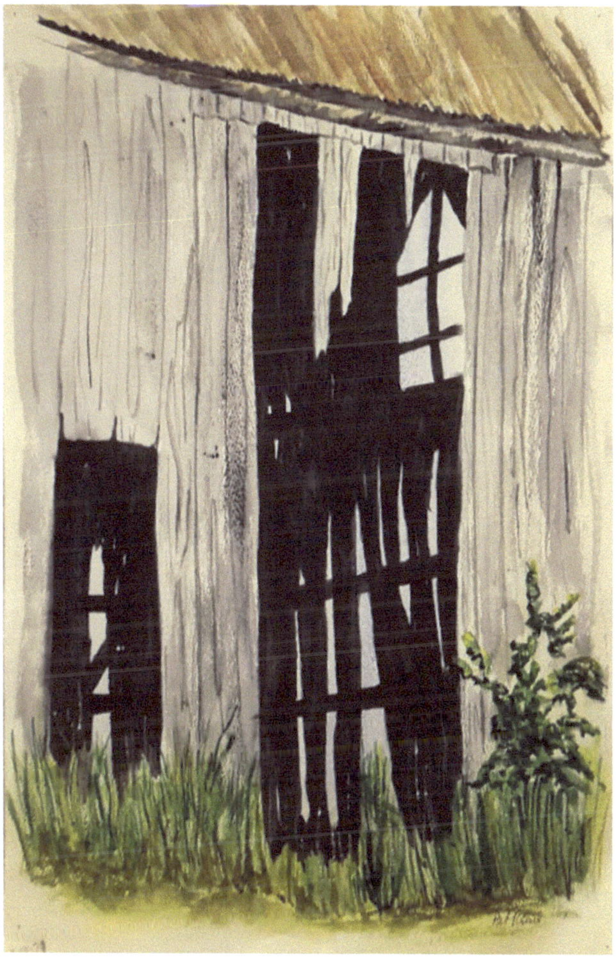

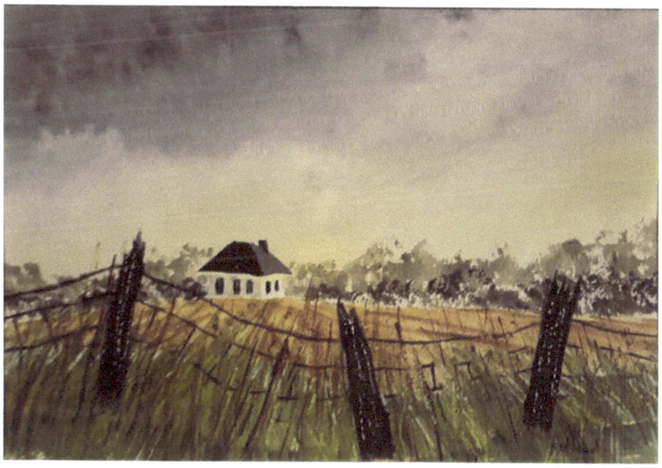

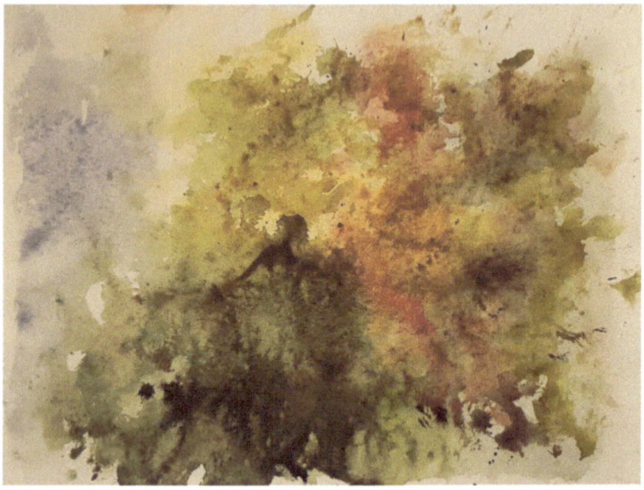

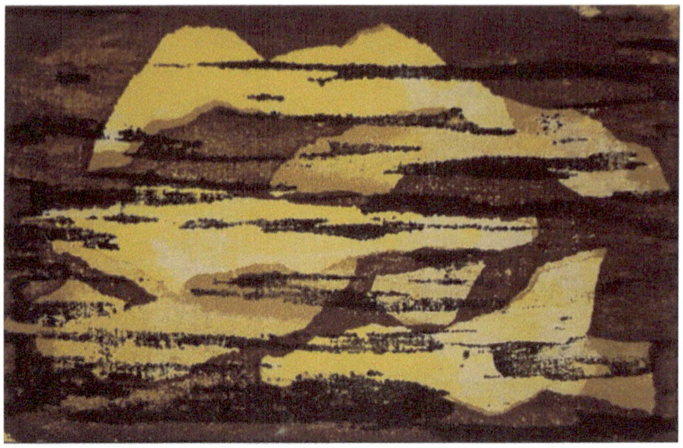

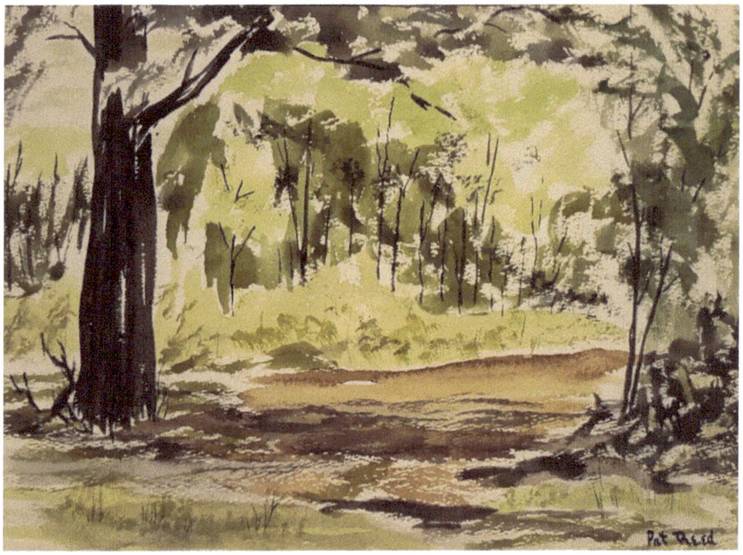
Pat Reed

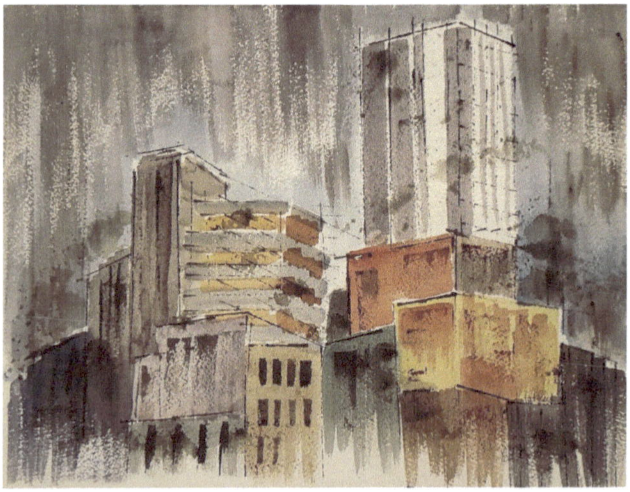

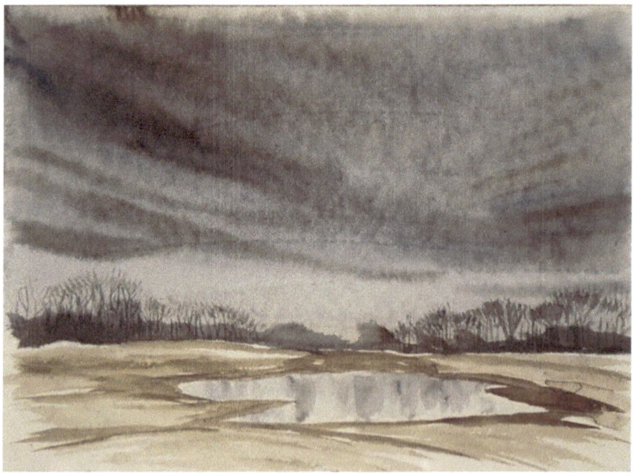

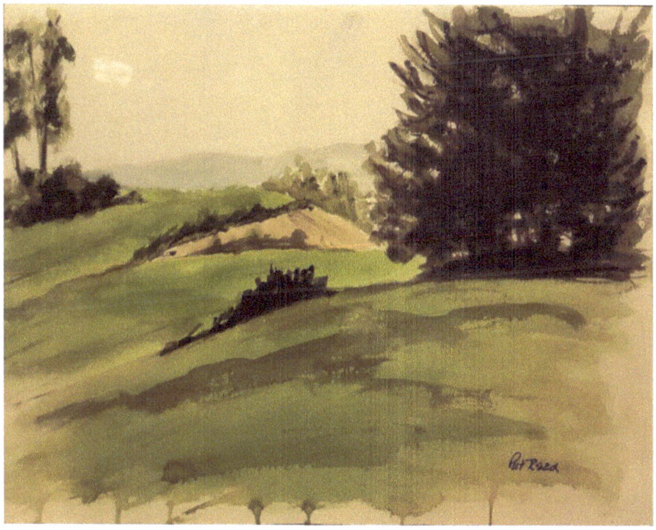

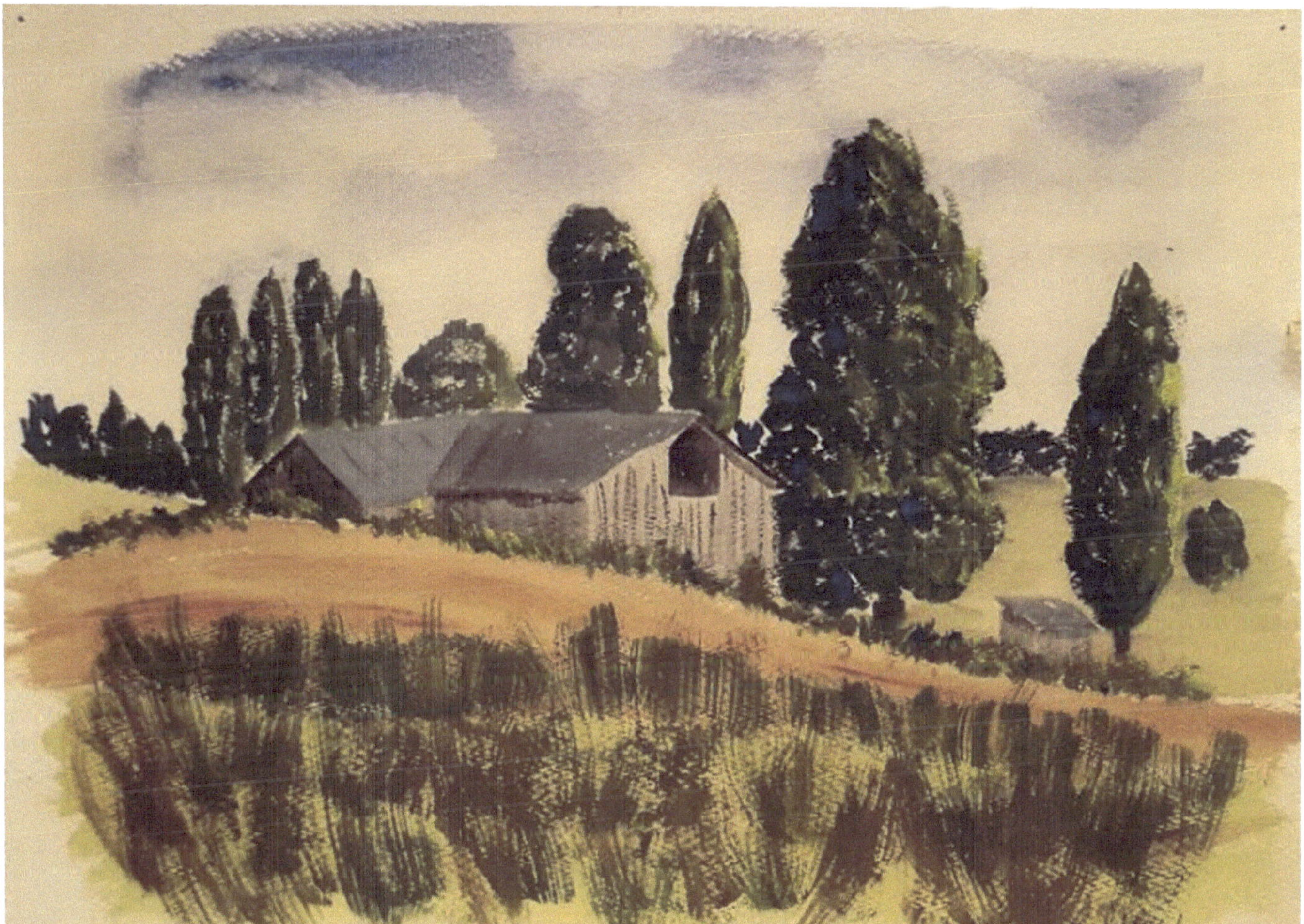

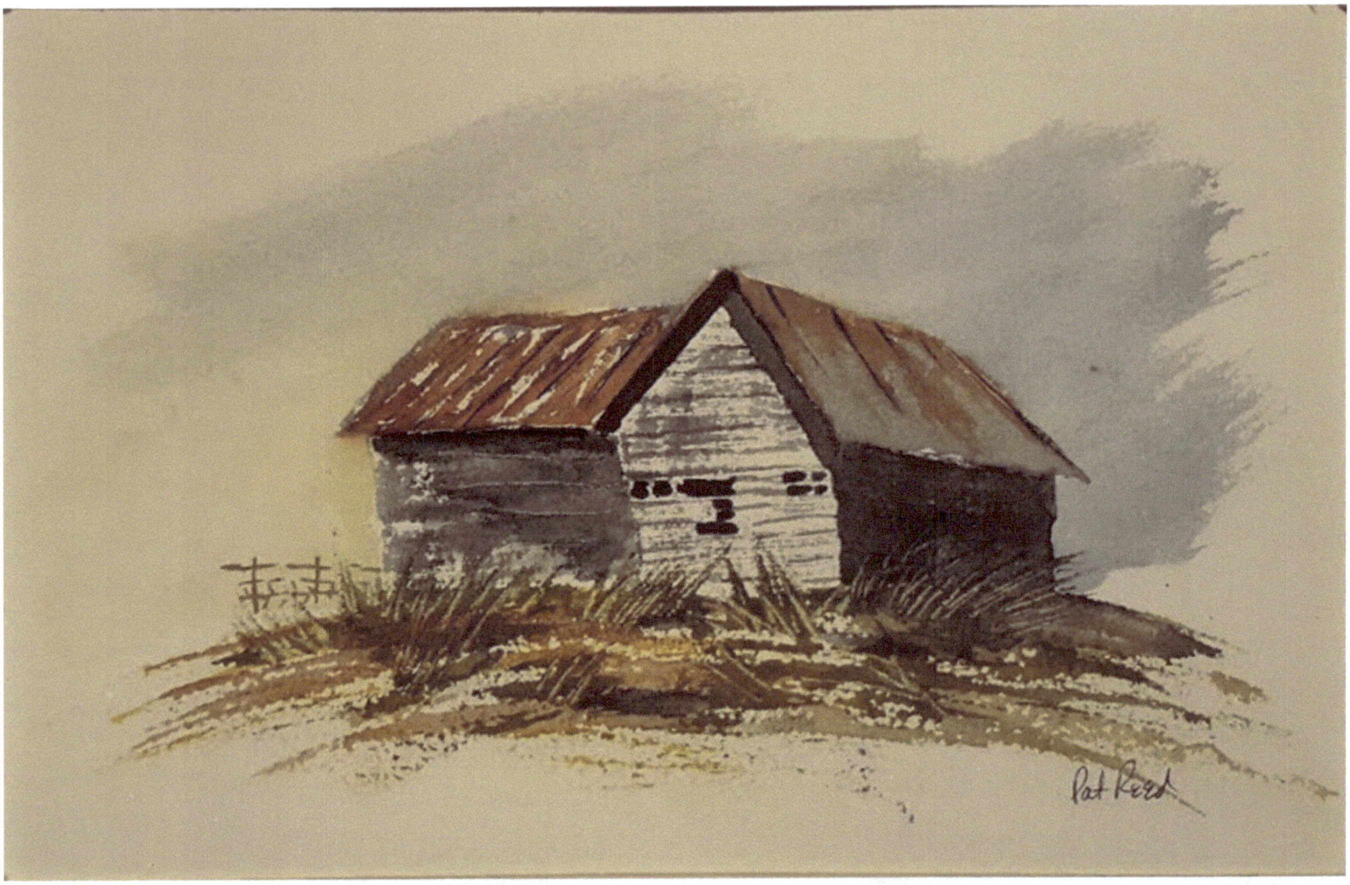
Pat Reed

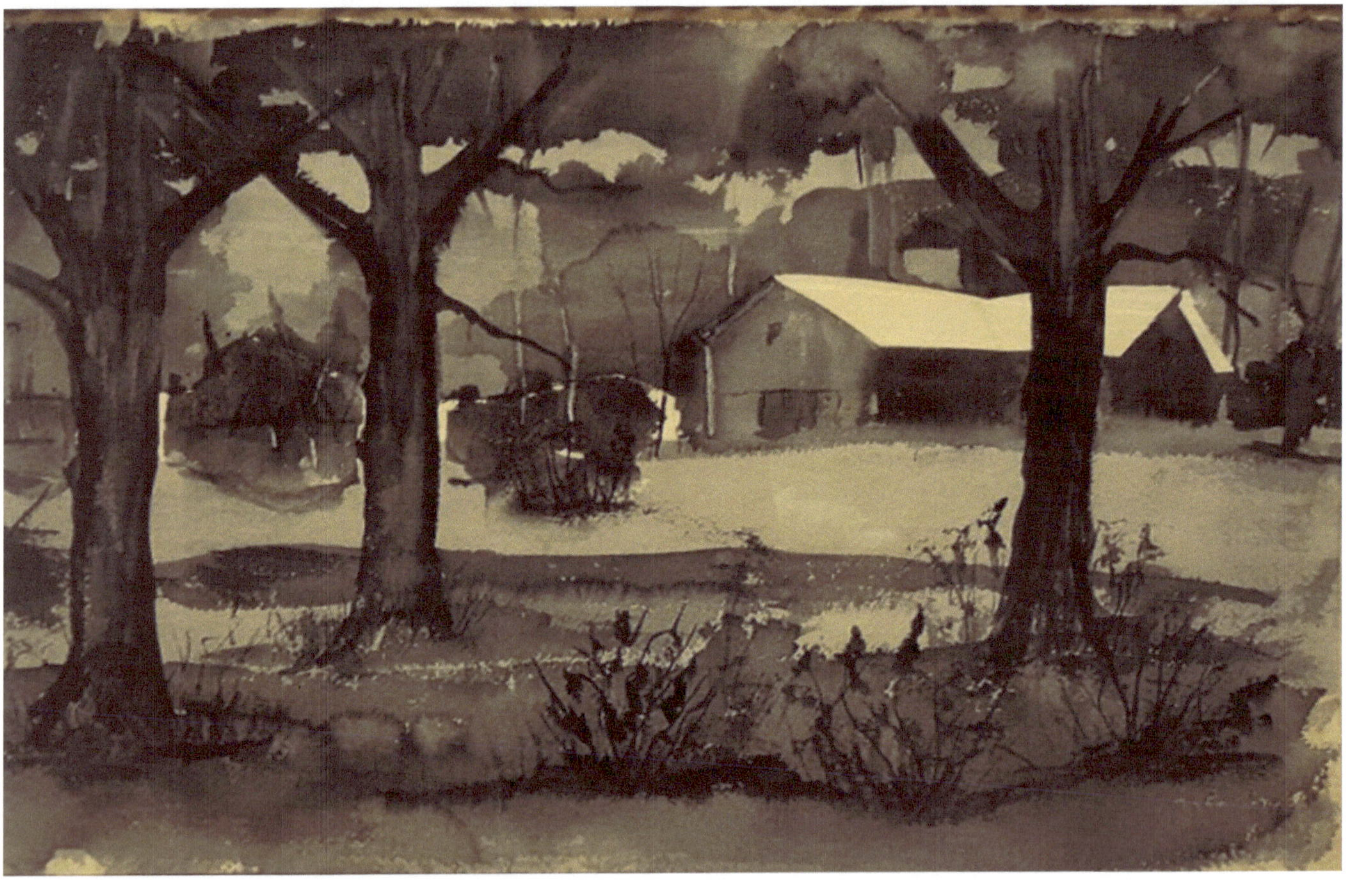

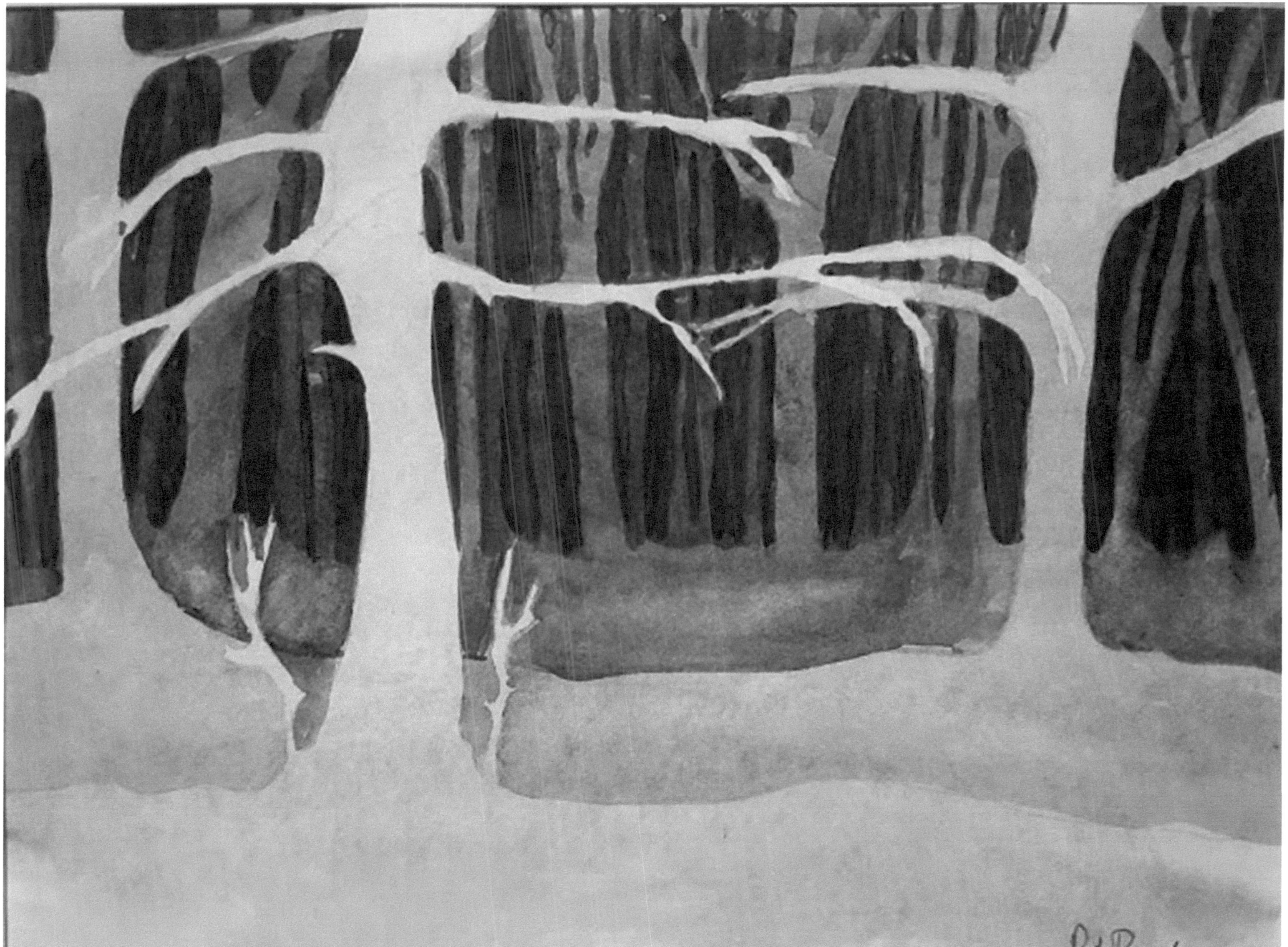
Pat Reed

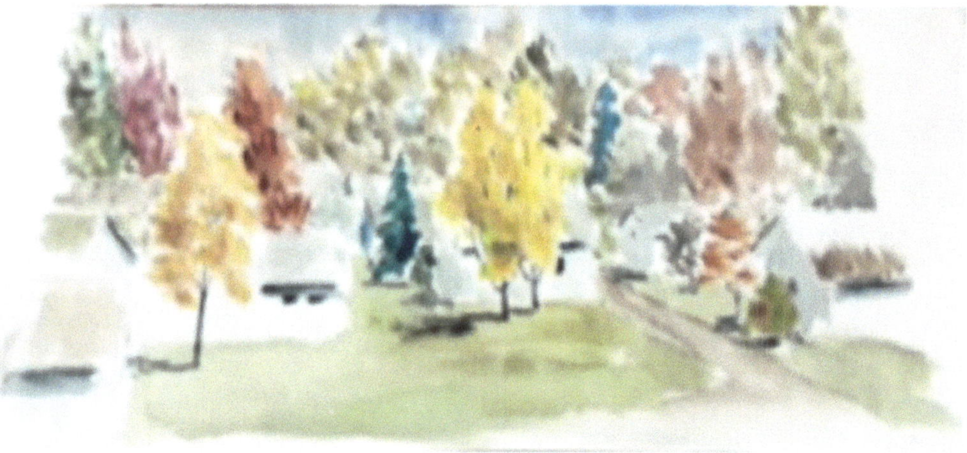

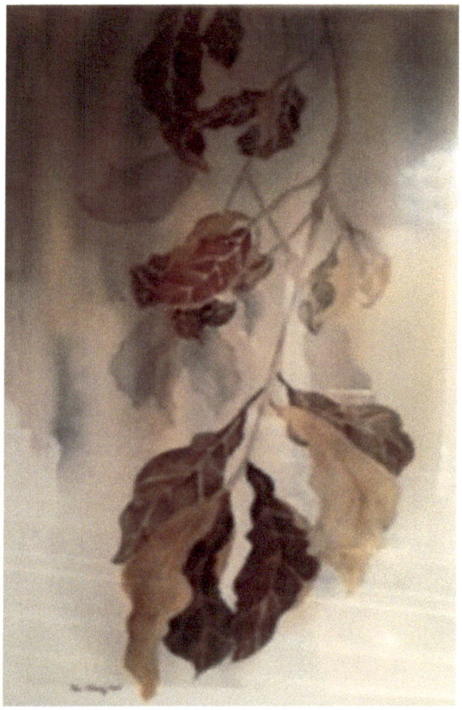

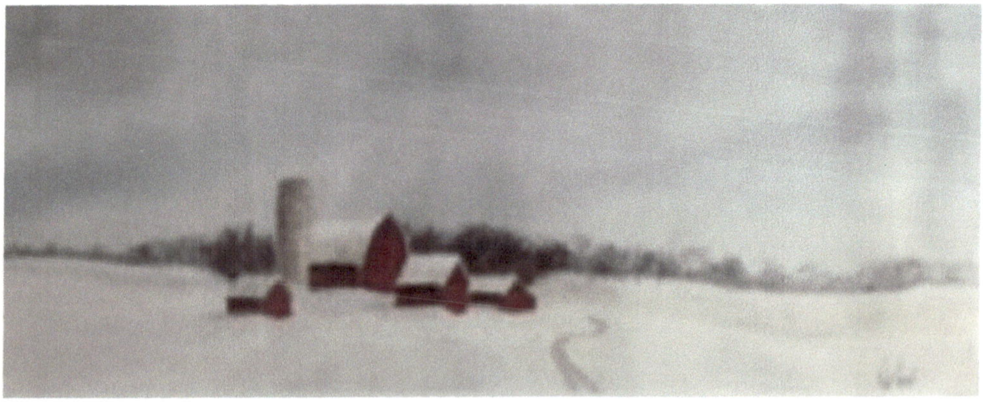

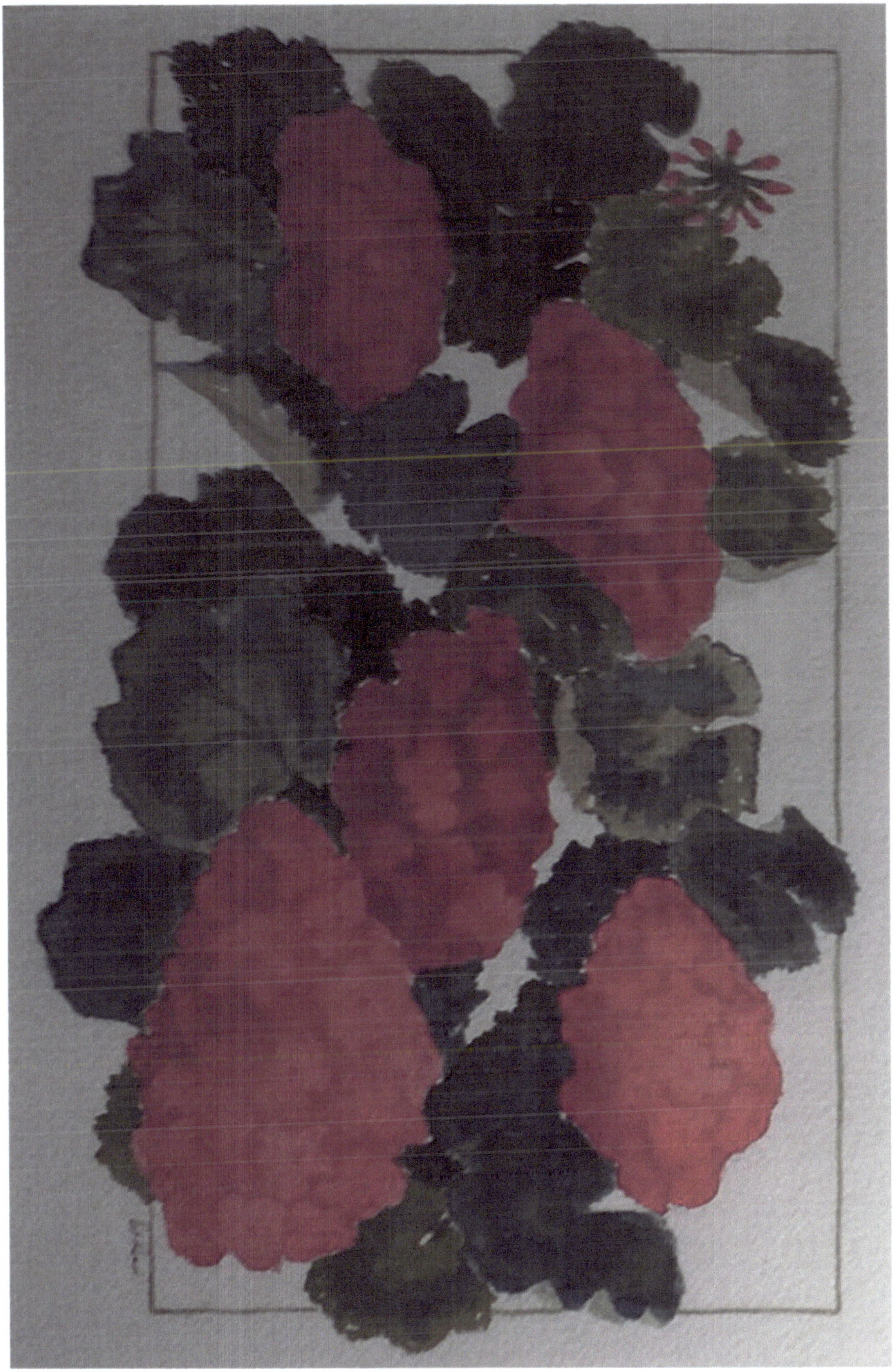

www.ingramcontent.com/pod-product-compliance
Lightning Source LLC
Chambersburg PA
CBHW050359180526
45159CB00005B/2077
9781540726032